IMAGES
of America

OXFORD AND
OLE MISS

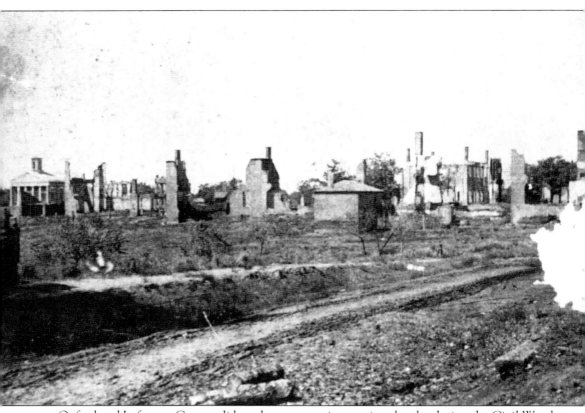

Oxford and Lafayette County did not have any major or minor battles during the Civil War, but on August 22, 1864, the war came to Oxford with a vengeance. While Gen. A. J. "Whiskey Joe" Smith was in Oxford, he ordered the burning of the downtown that included 35 buildings and five residences. This photograph is the only known photograph of the devastated town of Oxford. The building on the left-hand side is the Cumberland Presbyterian Church on South Street. The ladies of the local DAR chapter verified this photograph in the late 1930s as being a record of the "most devastated town in the South" during the Civil War. There is some dispute as to the authenticity of this photograph. (Courtesy of Patricia Brown Young Collection.)

ON THE COVER: Noted actor Will Geer portrayed the sheriff in the movie adaptation of William Faulkner's *Intruder in the Dust*. He is shown (second from left) at Heard's Feed Store just off the Courthouse Square behind city hall on East Jackson Avenue. The area is now a city-owned parking lot. (Courtesy of Patricia Brown Young Collection.)

IMAGES
of America

OXFORD AND
OLE MISS

Jack Lamar Mayfield on behalf of the
Oxford–Lafayette County Heritage Foundation

ARCADIA
PUBLISHING

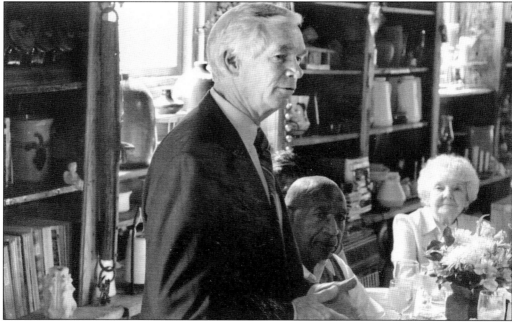

This publication is dedicated to the loving memory of Patricia Brown Young, who worked tirelessly throughout her lifetime for the preservation of the heritage of Oxford and Lafayette County. She was a charter member of the Oxford–Lafayette County Heritage Foundation (OLCHF) and served as the president of the foundation for many years. Shown in the picture with Brown are U.S. senator Thad Cochran and Oxford city alderman Preston Taylor (seated). The photograph was taken at the College Hill Store during the annual Christmas luncheon of the board of the OLCHF. Senator Cochran has been instrumental in securing funds for the restoration of the L. Q. C. Lamar Home and the Burns Belfry. (Courtesy of Bruce Newman/the *Oxford Eagle*.)

CONTENTS

ACKNOWLEDGMENTS

Most of the photographs in the publication were collected over the years by lifelong Oxford resident Patricia Brown Young. Her family members are among the first settlers in Oxford and Lafayette County. Unless otherwise noted, the photographs shown in this book are ones that she collected over a number of years. The photographs in chapter three are from the Special Collection Department of the University of Mississippi.

The Oxford Lafayette County Heritage Foundation also would like to acknowledge the assistance of Hilarie Pryor Bain, whose family has been in Oxford for the past seven generations, for assistance in the publication of this book. Also the assistance of many local foundation members and other Oxford citizens is greatly appreciated. My thanks go out to Will Lewis for correcting my mistakes and to James Pryor for the pictures of the Burns Belfry.

The author's proceeds from the sale of this publication will be used in the renovation of the Burns United Methodist Church. The church, also known as the Burns Belfry, is the first African American church established just after the Civil War by former slaves and is now a project of the OLCHF. The building, in later years, was owned by noted best-selling author John Grisham and was used as his office. Grisham donated the building to the OLCHF. When the building has been restored, it will be used by the people of Oxford and Lafayette County, particularly the poor. The foundation is now in the process of renovating the building.

INTRODUCTION

Our most illustrious resident, William Faulkner, was once asked what caused him to begin his Yoknapatawpha saga. His answer was what you might expect from the Nobel Laureate: "With 'Soldier's Pay' and 'Mosquitoes,' I wrote for the sake of writing because it was fun."

"Beginning with 'Sartoris,'" Faulkner went on to state, "I discovered my own little postage-stamp of native soil was worth writing about and that I would never live long enough to exhaust it."

Starting with the Chickasaw Cession in 1832—which opened up the Indian lands of north Mississippi for settlement and was partly the cause of the Trail of Tears—Oxford and Lafayette County were destined to become a crossroad of American history. The three pioneers—John Martin, John Chisom, and John Craig—purchased land from Princess Hoka in 1837, forming the City of Oxford, and had a plan to make Oxford a center of learning and culture for the old Southwest. These three men donated 50 acres of land that would be surveyed and laid out as the county seat of Lafayette County.

By 1841, the legislature of the state decided that the young men of Mississippi needed a place for higher learning. After several votes in the legislature, the new town of Oxford was selected as the home of the new state university. Two local businessmen each gave a half section of land to the state for the site of the University of Mississippi. Oxford had been given its name by one of the nephews of the three pioneer settlers, Dr. Thomas D. Isom, to entice legislators to vote for it as the location of the new state university.

In 1848, the University of Mississippi was opened for the enrollment of students, and for the next 160-plus years, Oxford and the university have been the scene of many events marking the progress of American history. This small town, like no other, has experienced some of the watersheds of the history of our nation. When you walk around our small Southern town, you understand what Faulkner meant when he stated he could not exhaust its history in his writings.

Examples of these events are many, but a few are named as follows: the removal of the Chickasaw Indians and the Trail of Tears, 1837; the formation of a great American public university, 1848; the invasion of Mississippi by Generals Grant and Sherman in an effort to capture Vicksburg in 1862; the burning of Oxford by Gen. "Whiskey Joe" Smith in retaliation for the raid on Fort Pillow by Gen. Nathan Bedford Forrest (other historians state it was because of Forrest's raid on Memphis or because of the burning of Chambersburg, Pennsylvania, by Confederate forces), 1864; reconciliation between the North and South during Reconstruction by men such as Oxford resident and statesman L. Q. C. Lamar, 1870s; the "last battle of the Civil War" and the integration of Ole Miss in 1962; and the first presidential debate between Senators McCain and Obama, 2008.

Oxford has now become a mecca for retiring baby boomers and a hot spot for second homes and weekend destinations. We have much to offer these weekend visitors or people looking for a retirement home. "My little postage-stamp of native soil," as Faulkner stated, is not only worth writing about, it is also worth exploring and experiencing. The way of life in a small Southern town has no better example than that of Oxford, Mississippi.

The Oxford–Lafayette County Heritage Foundation was formed more than 10 years ago to preserve and protect the heritage of our town. The last chapter of this publication gives an example of the work carried on by the foundation. We have completed the $2-million renovation of the home of statesman L. Q. C. Lamar and are now in the process of renovating the first African American church in Oxford.

If you would like to make a tax-deductible donation for the renovation of this historic building, you may do so to the Oxford–Lafayette County Heritage Foundation, a 501c nonprofit organization, P.O. Box 622, Oxford, MS 38655.

One

THE LAFAYETTE COUNTY COURTHOUSE

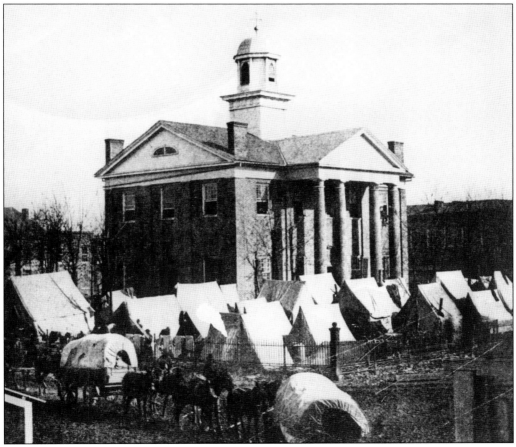

When Oxford was formed in 1837, fifty acres were donated to the county for a site for the county seat. These 50 acres were laid out in a street and building site grid in the geographical center of the county. This grid pattern was laid out by the maternal great-grandfather of William Faulkner, Charles Butler. Acreage was set aside for the construction of a jail and courthouse, and the other acreage was sold for the construction of these two buildings. The first courthouse was constructed and occupied by late 1840. On August 22, 1864, this courthouse was burned by the invading Union Army. Yankee tents are shown on the grounds of the courthouse before its destruction. This is the only photograph remaining of the original Lafayette County Courthouse.

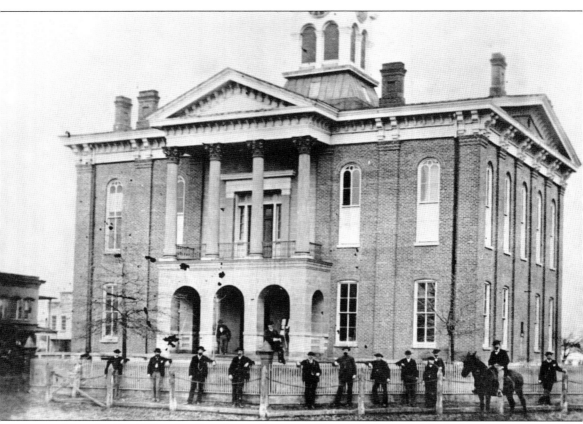

After the Civil War, the Courthouse Square and business district of Oxford were reconstructed by 1872. The current courthouse that now stands in the central business district is somewhat different from the first courthouse. It has a four-faced clock on the top of the building, and the columns go down to archways and not to the ground. William Faulkner gives a description of both courthouses in his novel *Requiem for a Nun*.

The second Lafayette County Courthouse was constructed on the foundation of the previous building. This first courthouse was constructed in a grove of oak trees that were destroyed by the invading Yankees. This photograph, from the late 1870s, is a winter scene showing the new-growth trees covered in ice.

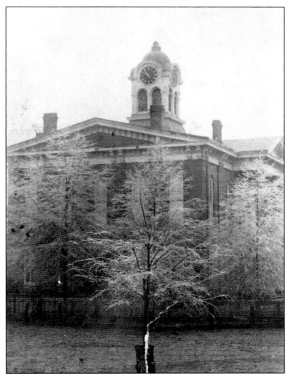

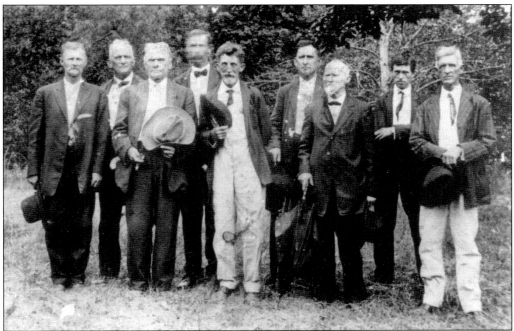

This turn-of-the-20th-century photograph shows some of the courthouse employees and county officials. Among those pictured are Tom Metts (far right), the Lafayette County sheriff, and Guy McLarty (second from right), the circuit clerk.

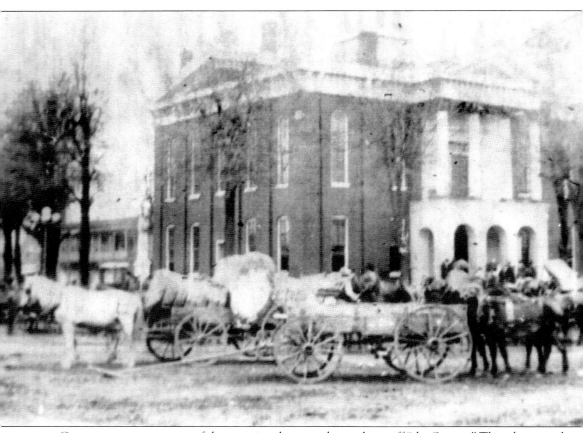

Cotton wagons go to one of the two gins that were located just off "the Square." This photograph was taken from the northeast corner of the Square, and just to the left, note the 1907 Civil War Monument. For many years, these two cotton gins were in service on the east side of the Square. Today there is only one gin operating in the county, near Taylor.

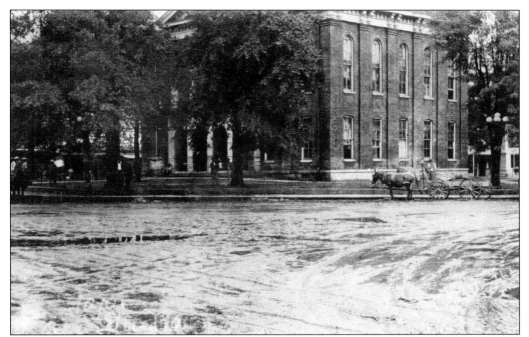

This is a view of the courthouse from the northwest corner of the Square. This photograph dates to between 1907, when the Civil War Monument was dedicated, and the early 1920s, when the Square was paved. Note the monument on the right side of the photograph.

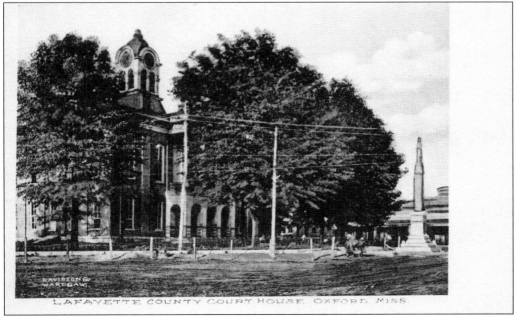

LAFAYETTE COUNTY COURT HOUSE OXFORD MISS

This view of the Lafayette County Courthouse is a postcard from around the beginning of the 20th century. Note that at the lower left-hand corner of the postcard is the name Davidson and Wardlaw. This was a stationary shop in Oxford. The image dates to after 1907 and before the early 1920s.

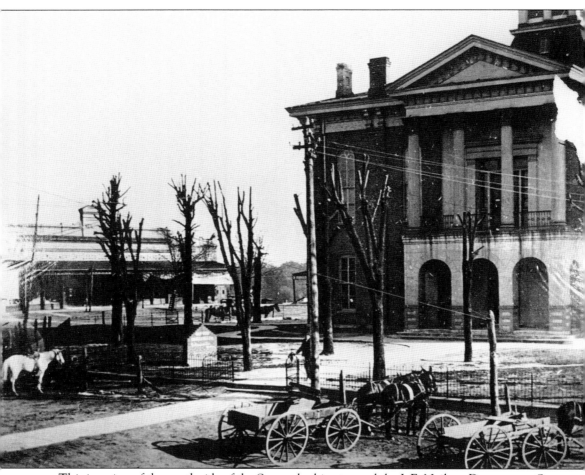

This is a view of the north side of the Square looking toward the J. E. Neilson Department Store. Note that the horses and mules are tethered to the hitching posts around the courthouse. Also note the power lines and post in the courtyard. A number of the photographs in the Patricia Brown Young Collection were made to showcase new Oxford power lines.

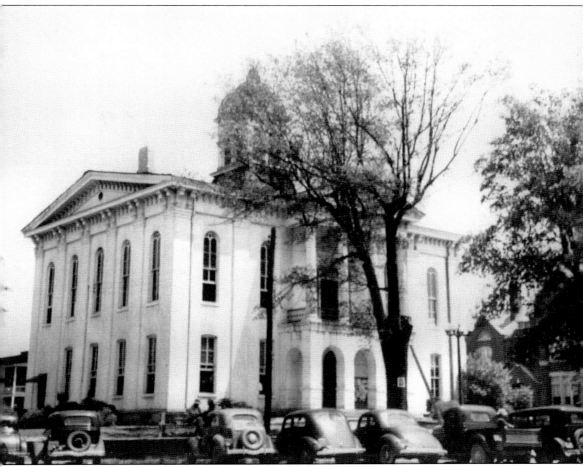

This view of the courthouse is from the early 1930s with the Federal Building in the right-hand background. The stucco has been applied to the brick exterior of the building.

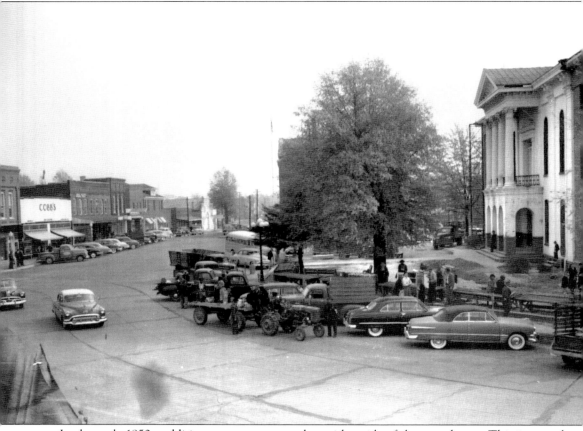

In the early 1950s, additions were constructed on either side of the courthouse. This is a north side view of the building, and one can see on the right side of the building that the new brickwork has not had stucco applied to the exterior. Also note Cobbs Dry Goods Store, which has been replaced by the present-day First National Bank.

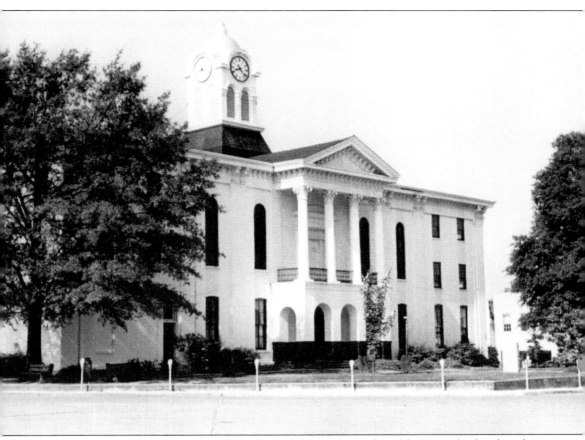

The north side view of the courthouse from the early 1950s shows the additions to both sides of the building. The stucco has now been applied to the building. This view is similar to what one would see today on the Square but without the parking meters.

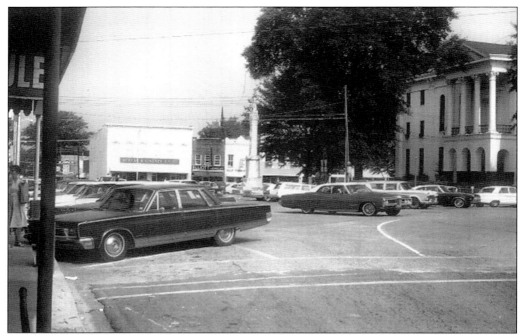

This is a view of the west side of the Square from the mid-1960s. Note the buildings that were on the southwest corner of the town square. This photograph also shows a corner of the Golden Rule 5-and-10-Cent Store. (Courtesy of Lauren Childress.)

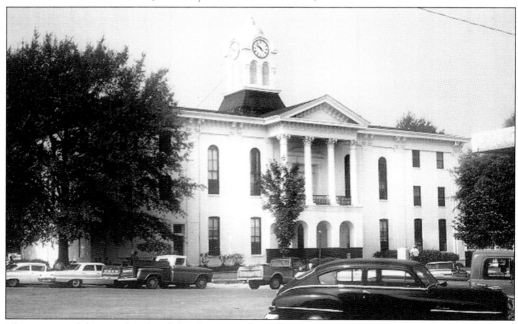

This image of the north side of the Square is from the same time as the above photograph. This was the side of the Square where the truck farmers would park their pickups and sell produce during the summer months. Local residents would pull alongside the farmers and purchase their fresh farm-raised produce. (Courtesy of Lauren Childress.)

Two

HISTORIC DOWNTOWN OXFORD

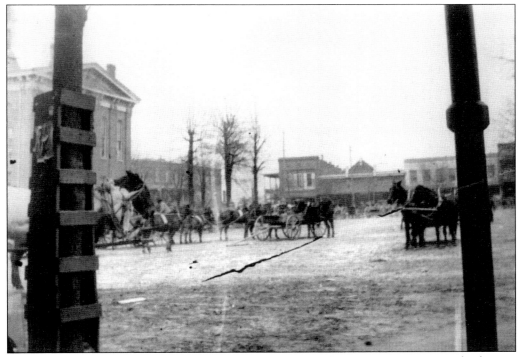

In this view of the Square from the early 1890s, the mule-drawn wagons are going both ways around the Square. Up until World War II, one could navigate the Square in any direction. There were trees planted around the area in front of the stores; they no longer exist. Boards were placed around the trees to keep the mules and horses from rubbing against the trees and removing the bark. Sometimes the mules chewed the bark off the trees.

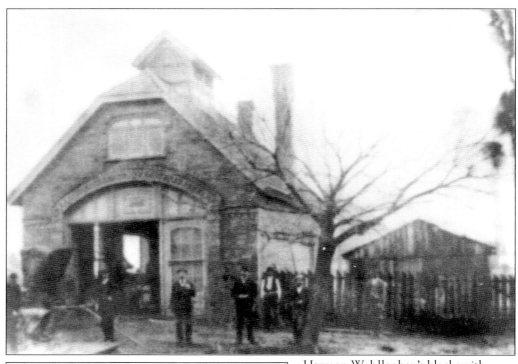

Herman Wohllenben's blacksmith shop was on South Lamar Boulevard in the area of the present-day restaurant Proud Larry's just across Harrison Avenue. "Ole Bully" and his wife, Katrina, came to Oxford in the 1850s and opened his shop. This photograph is from around 1880. He and his wife had five daughters, four of whom married into well-known Oxford families. The fifth daughter died in early childhood. They were considered the "most beautiful ladies in town." The daughers were Minnie Carter, Bell Neilson, Emma Sultan, Lillie Hudson, and Bessie Cobb.

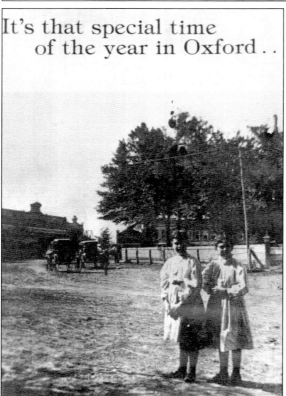

One of Ole Bully's daughters, Bell, married J. E. Neilson, the son of the founder of Neilson's Department Store. Neilson's is in the background in this view of the Square from the early part of the 20th century. This photograph was used in an advertisement from Neilson's.

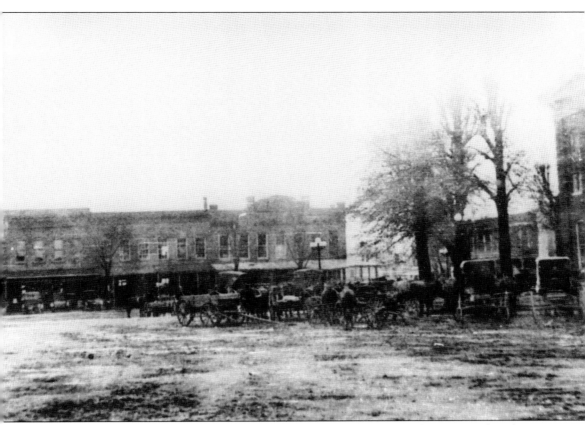

This is a 1910 view of the southeast side of the Square and the businesses there. Note that the horse- and mule-drawn wagons are around the hitching posts on the courthouse grounds and the automobiles are on the store side of the Square. The Confederate monument can be seen on the right-hand side of the photograph.

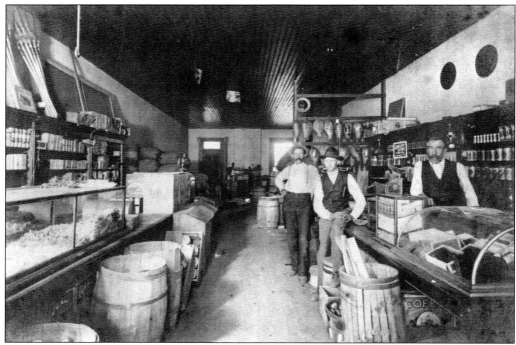

The interior of E. H. Kimmons's grocery store is pictured here around 1900. Kimmons is the man behind the counter.

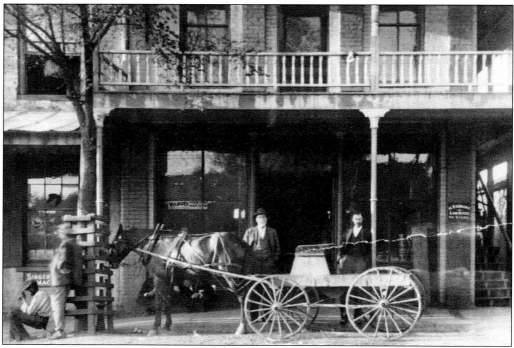

A Square scene from about 1900 on the northeast side of the Square shows the building that is now occupied by Duvall's, next to the First National Bank.

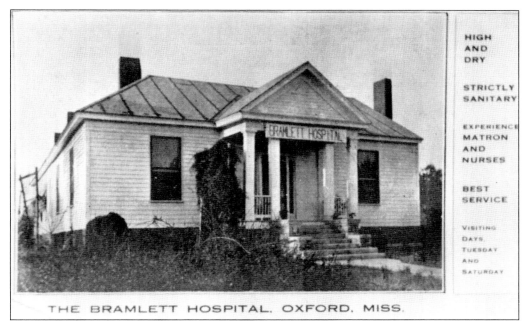

THE BRAMLETT HOSPITAL, OXFORD, MISS.

During the first half of the 20th century, Oxford had two hospitals. One was owned by Dr. J. C. Culley and was located west of the Square on Van Buren Avenue. It has now been replaced by condominiums. The other hospital was on Madison Avenue just to the northeast of the Square. It was owned by Dr. E. S. Bramlett. Dr. Bramlett's hospital also had a nursing school for licensed practical nurses.

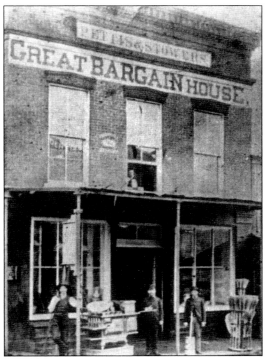

Pettis and Stowers Hardware Store was located on the northwest side of the Square. This view is from about 1880. The building was later Lewis and McKee Hardware and today is Rooster's.

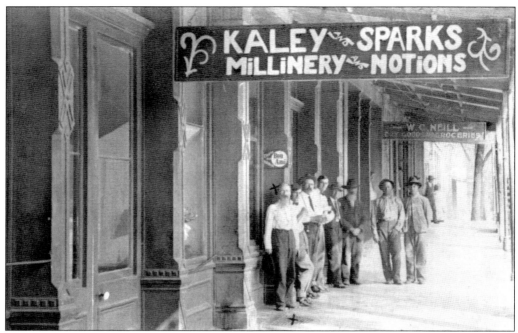

W. C. Neil's Dry Goods and Grocery Store was located on the northeast side of the Square. Neil is the man with the long beard standing on the far left. The store was near the present-day SouthBank.

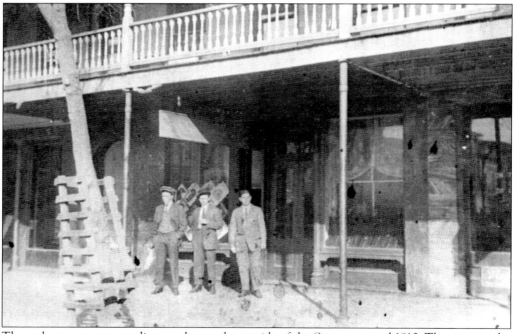

These three men are standing on the northwest side of the Square around 1910. The man on the left is Earle Moore, and the man on the right is Shaw Robinson. The other man is unidentified. This is where the Downtown Grill is today and was once Thomas Dudley Isom's drugstore.

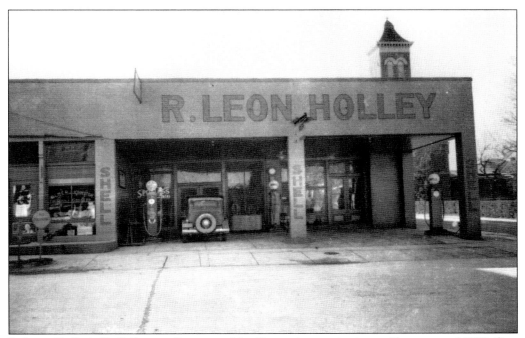

R. Leon Holley's Shell Service Station on Van Buren Avenue is pictured here around 1930. One can see the steeple of the First Presbyterian Church in the background. The business was located on the present-day site of Mississippi Madness, just west of the Lyric.

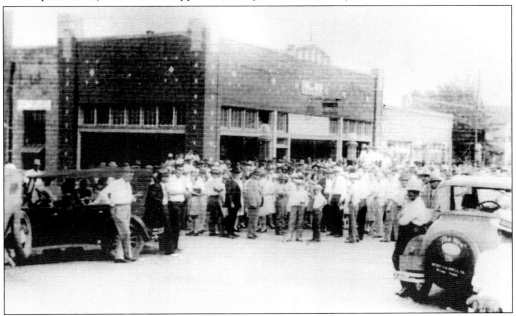

This Ford car dealership operated in the early 1930s on South Lamar Boulevard. The reason there are so many people in front of the building is that the dealership was having a drawing for a free giveaway of a new car. This building is located on the east side of the street across from Holli's Sweet Tooth.

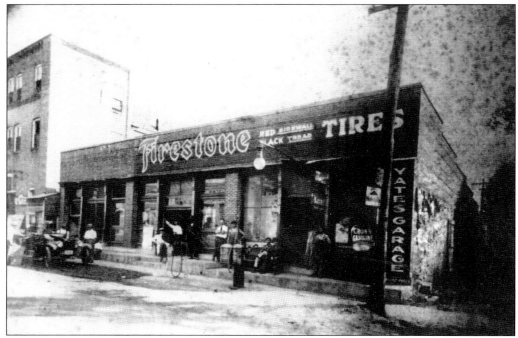

This tire dealership was on West Van Buren Avenue next to the Lyric. Note the Lyric has three stories. The top story was later destroyed by fire. At this time, the Lyric was known as the Oxford Opera House.

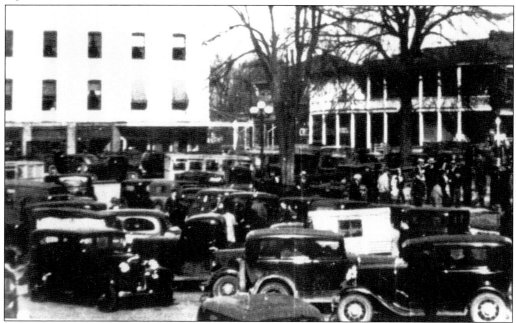

Here is a Saturday on the Square in downtown Oxford. This is the west side of the Square looking toward the present-day Thompson House. Notice the cars are going both ways in this early-1930s photograph.

The front of the Lyric Theatre in the 1940s is shown here. The third floor is missing. This photograph was taken sometime after the fire that destroyed the top floor.

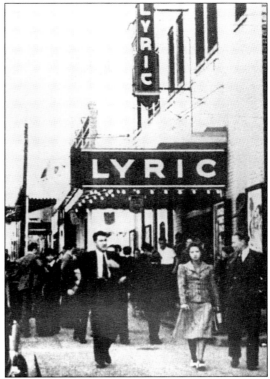

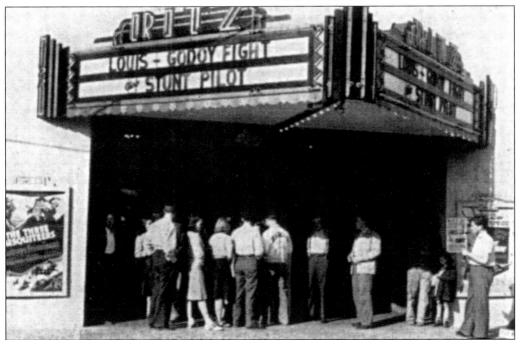

Oxford's other movie theater, the Ritz, opened after the Lyric. The Ritz Building is now condos on the north side of West Van Buren Avenue.

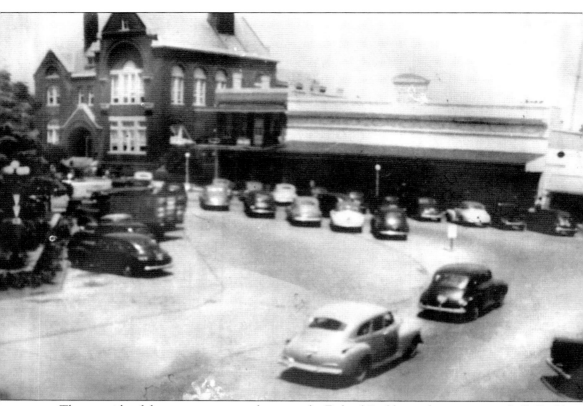

The east side of the town square was home to the Federal Building, what is now city hall, Ruth's ladies' dress shop, and Neilson's Department Store. The Neilson's store building was constructed about 1899. The business was formed in 1839. The oldest department store in the South and the 16th oldest department store in the United States, Neilson's had been on all sides of the Square at different times. This photograph dates to the late 1940s.

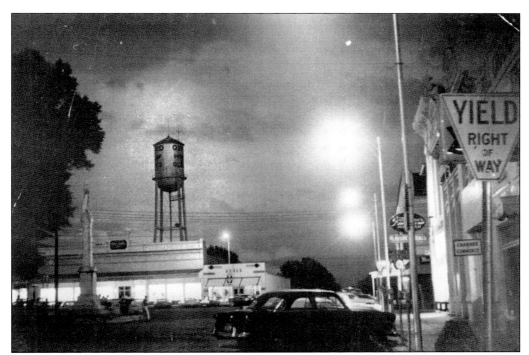

Neilson's Department Store is pictured at twilight. Note Blaylock's Drug Store and the Fortune Ice Cream sign. This is the building that now houses the nationally known Square Books.

This photograph of the north side of the Square looking to the east was taken next to where the present-day Downtown Grill is located, just past the barber's pole on Parks Barber Shop. These different businesses are no longer on the Square.

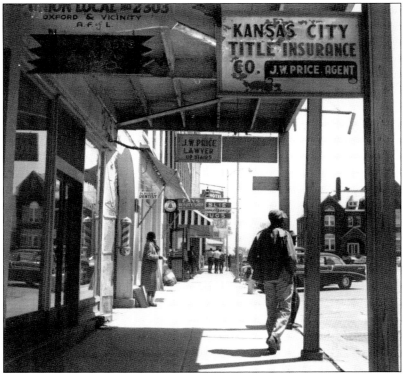

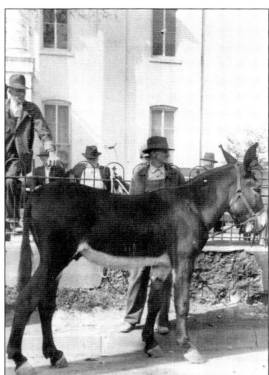

The fenced area of the Square has been used for many things over the years. This photograph from the late 1930s shows a mule trader similar to what one would read about in the Snopes family trilogy: *The Hamlet*, *The Town*, and *The Mansion*.

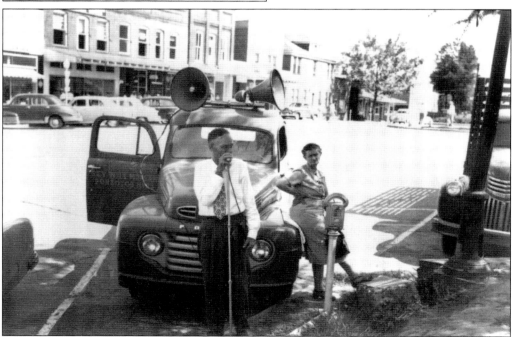

Political speeches, "Welcome Rebel" parties, truck farmers, mule traders, and even itinerant preachers were known to use the area next to the courthouse. This photograph is looking toward east Jackson Avenue and the location of the O. H. Douglas Funeral Home (center).

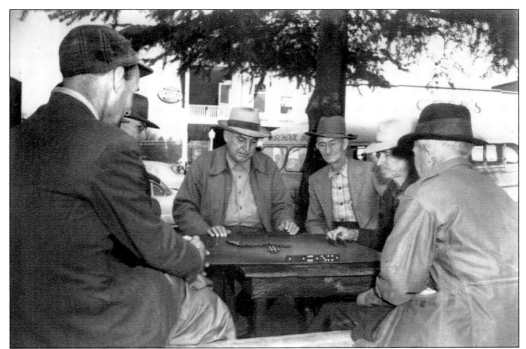

At one time, the grounds of the courthouse had tables where local men would get up a domino game. This was on the north side of the Square looking toward North Lamar Boulevard.

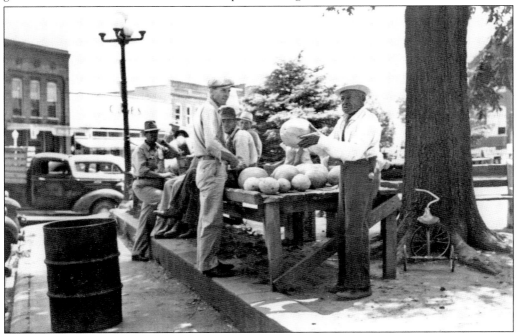

On the north side of the courthouse grounds were two long wooden tables. Truck farmers would use them to sell watermelons and cantaloupes. The tables sat in the present-day fenced-in area where the air-conditioning units are now housed.

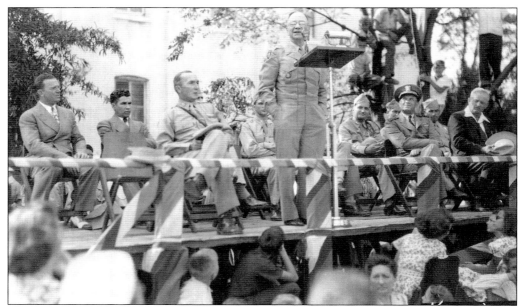

Lt. Gen. Daniel Isom Sultan makes a speech on the west side of the courthouse grounds in 1946 shortly before his death. Sultan, who was a grandson of "Ole Bully" Wohllenben, left Oxford and attended West Point. He was on Gen. Joseph Stillwell's staff during World War II and later became the commander of the Burma/Southeast Asia theater during the war. To the far left of Sultan are Congressman Jamie L. Whitten and city attorney Bramlett Roberts. (Courtesy of Will Lewis.)

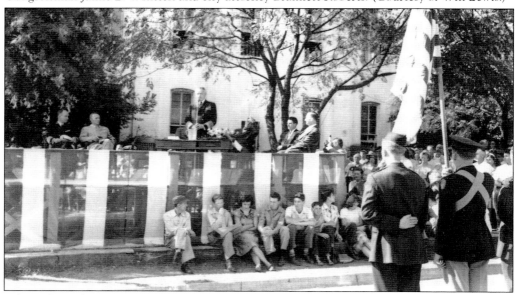

Adm. John Sidney McCain, the grandfather of Sen. John McCain, attended the University of Mississippi before going to the Naval Academy. Admiral McCain was from Carollton, Mississippi. Vice Admiral William F. "Bull" Halsey came to Oxford for the dedication of McCain Hall, which would later become the Barnard Observatory and the home of the Center for the Study of Southern Culture. Halsey made a speech on the west side of the courthouse grounds shortly after the death of Admiral McCain. (Courtesy of Will Lewis.)

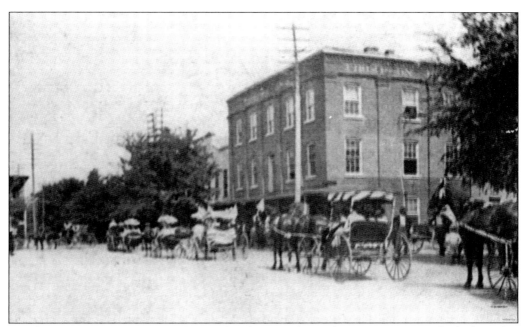

Confederate Memorial Day is celebrated with a parade on the Square in 1910 Oxford. In this photograph, the decorated carriages are heading toward Jackson Avenue with the Thompson House in the background. Note the poles that were in use at the time for telephone, telegraph, and electrical power.

Local Oxford resident Charles Sisk has his favorite horse decked out for the Confederate Memorial Day Parade in 1910. This photograph also shows the Thompson House in the background.

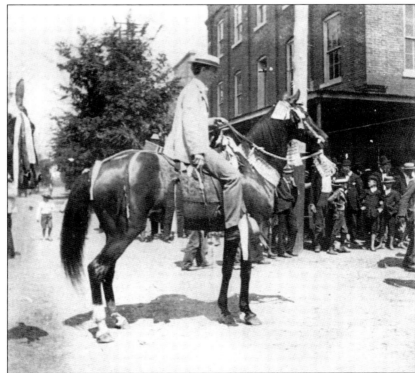

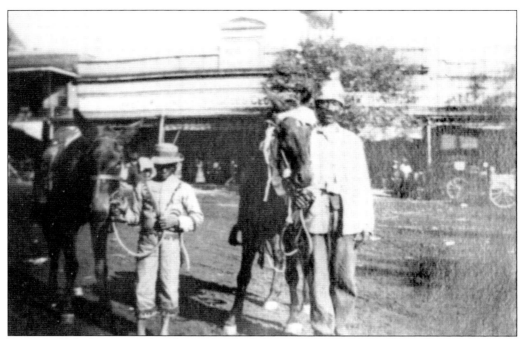

Porters hold the horse reins for riders in the Confederate Memorial Day Parade. Neilson's Department Store is shown in the background.

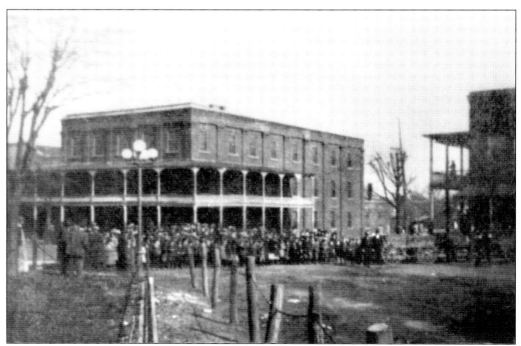

A crowd of Oxford and Lafayette County residents gathers in front of the Thompson House for the Confederate Memorial Day Parade in 1910.

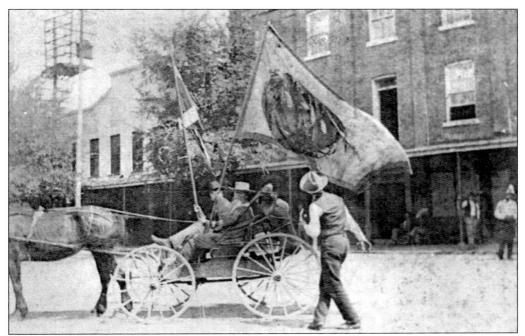

Confederate veterans of the Lafayette Guards drive onto the southeast corner of the Square off South Lamar Boulevard. Note that the veterans have their company battle flag, presented to the group by the ladies of Oxford at a ceremony at the Cumberland Presbyterian Church in 1861.

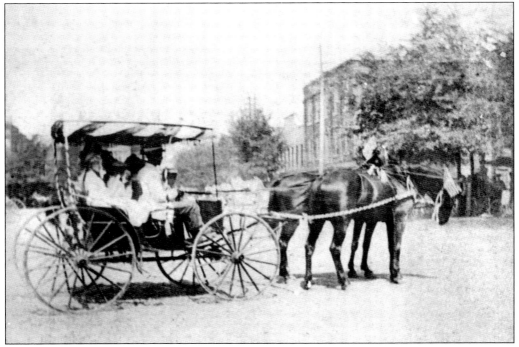

Participants in the 1910 Confederate Memorial Day Parade are driven around the Square in their decorated carriage. This parade was held for many years after the Civil War.

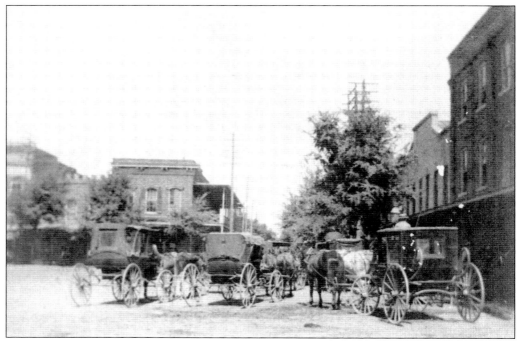

Oxford residents leave the Square after the 1910 Confederate Memorial Day Parade. They take the same route down Jackson Avenue off the Square at the end of the event as did the parade participants.

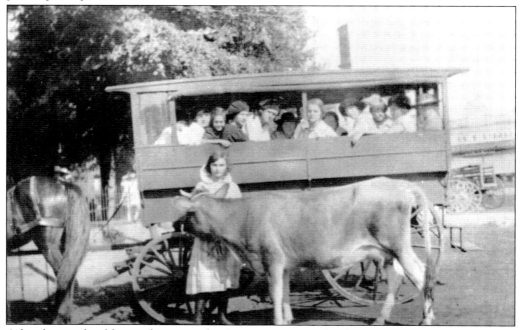

A local city school bus is shown on the Square in 1914. Why the cow is beside the students is unknown. Maybe they were taking the cow to the public school just off the Square on Jackson Avenue so they could have fresh milk with their lunch.

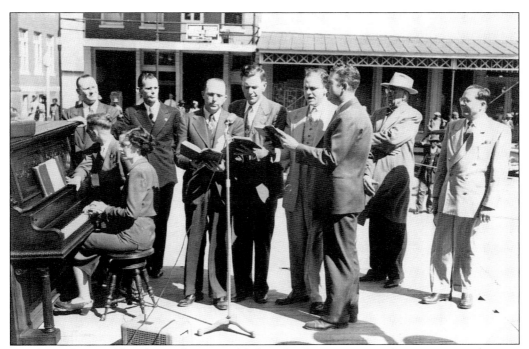

Local First Baptist Church members assembled on the Square to sing religious songs and garner support and attendance for a revival. The man in the hat is the pastor of the church, Dr. Frank Moody Purser. The photograph dates from the early 1950s.

This is the audience that gathered on the Square for the 1950s rally in support of a revival at the First Baptist Church. The gathering is on the east side of the courthouse, which was used for political rallies and to listen to Ole Miss football games broadcasted by the local AM radio station, WSUH.

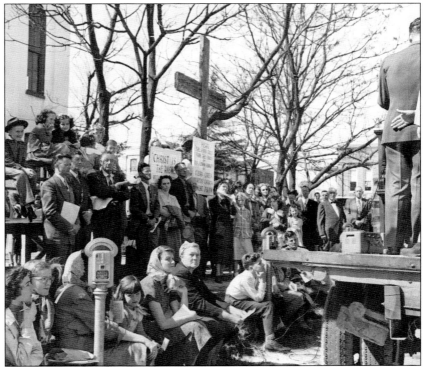

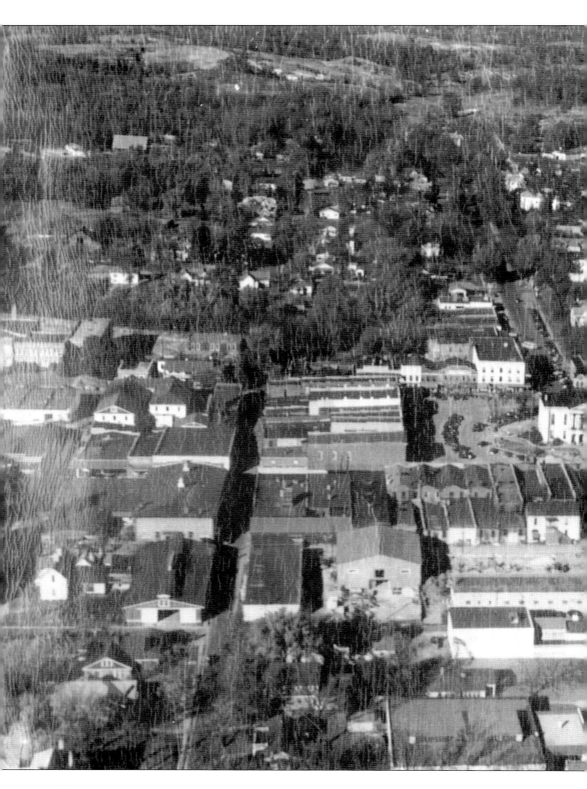

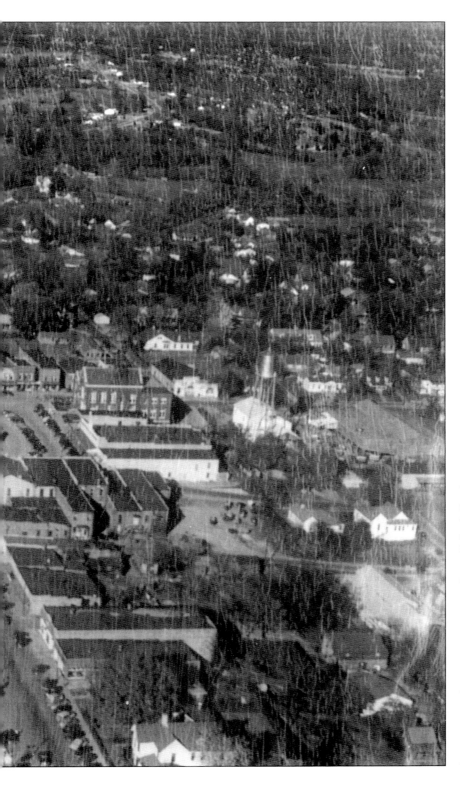

This is
an aerial
view of
downtown
Oxford and
the town
square from
1948. Note
that the
additional
wings have
not been
added
to the
courthouse.
Look
around
and see
what has
changed.

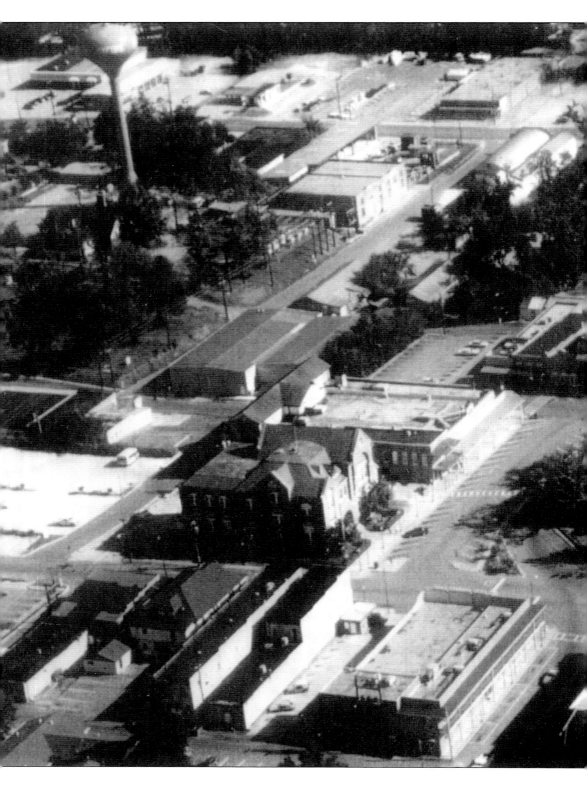

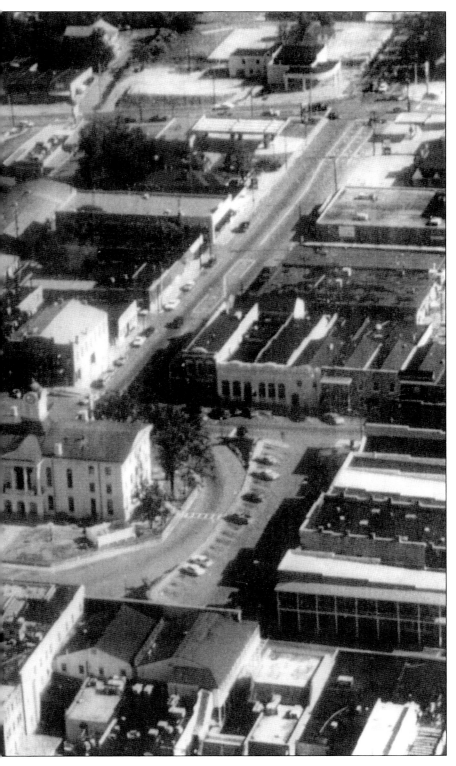

This is an aerial view of downtown Oxford from 1978. Local hardware store owner Harry Sneed took this photograph from his personal aircraft.

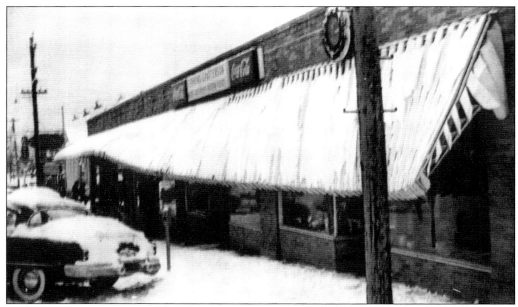

Oxford residents experienced a rather large snowfall in the early 1960s. This snowfall amounted to a little more than 16 inches, which was unusual for Oxford. This is the block of buildings that replaced the old Cumberland Presbyterian Church on South Lamar Boulevard when it was torn down in 1941. This building is in the current area of Pearl Street Pasta restaurant and Cat Daddy's T-shirt store.

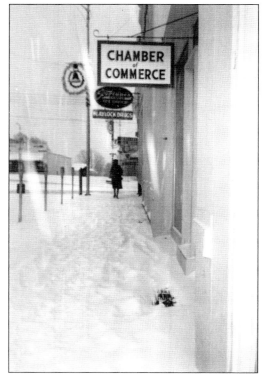

The snowstorm of the early 1960s is shown on the southeast side of the Square. The Blaylock's Drug Store sign is shown in the photograph. This is the location of the present-day Square Books, and the chamber of commerce was above the present-day City Grocery.

Three

THE HISTORIC UNIVERSITY OF MISSISSIPPI, OLE MISS

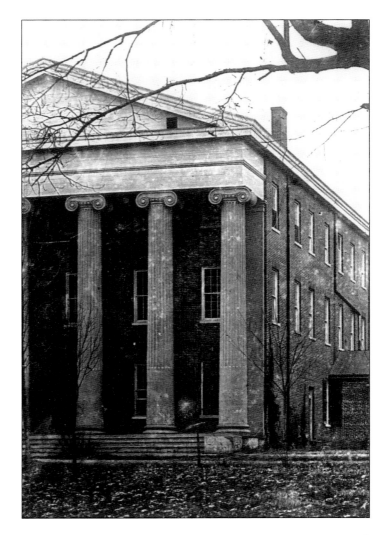

The Lyceum was the first building constructed on the University of Mississippi campus. It was designed by architect William Nichols, who is considered the "architect of the Old South." Nichols also designed the first capitol building for Mississippi and many other public buildings in North Carolina, Alabama, and Louisiana.

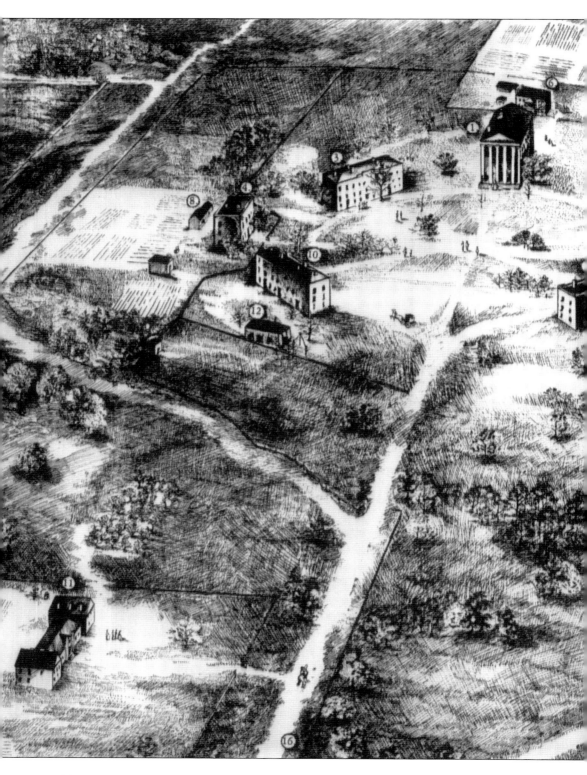

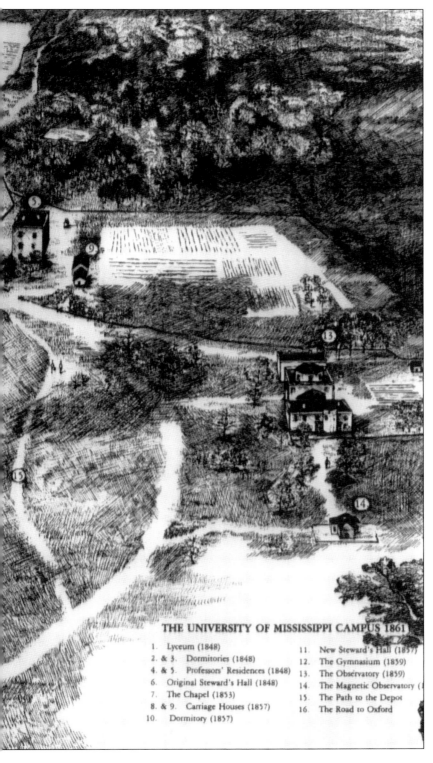

THE UNIVERSITY OF MISSISSIPPI CAMPUS 1861

1. Lyceum (1848)
2. & 3. Dormitories (1848)
4. & 5. Professors' Residences (1848)
6. Original Steward's Hall (1848)
7. The Chapel (1853)
8. & 9. Carriage Houses (1857)
10. Dormitory (1857)
11. New Steward's Hall (1857)
12. The Gymnasium (1859)
13. The Observatory (1859)
14. The Magnetic Observatory (
15. The Path to the Depot
16. The Road to Oxford

The University of Mississippi campus was designed to be situated around a central area. The map was drawn by Deborah J. T. Freeland. This map depicts all of the buildings and their locations on the campus prior to 1861. No buildings on the campus were destroyed when the City of Oxford was burned on August 22, 1864, because they had been used by the Union forces for war hospital purposes.

45

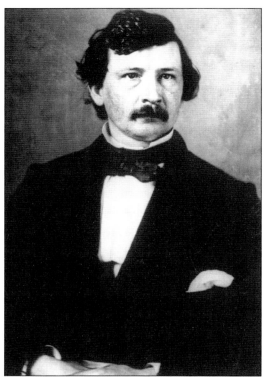

Edward Carlisle Boynton is responsible for the photographs that exist today of the campus prior to the Civil War. Boynton came to the university as professor of chemistry, mineralogy, and geology in 1856. He was an amateur photographer and made all of the photographs that survive the war. When he left the university at the beginning of the war to return to the North, he left his negatives on campus in the observatory and planned to return to the campus after the war to retrieve his property. Boynton never returned to Oxford after the war.

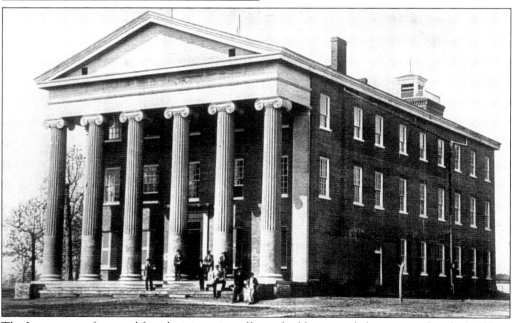

The Lyceum was first used for administrative offices, the library, and classrooms after the building was constructed in 1848. During the Civil War, the building was used, at various times, by both Union and Confederate forces for a hospital. Today the building houses the offices of the chancellor and other university administration offices. It is the oldest building on campus.

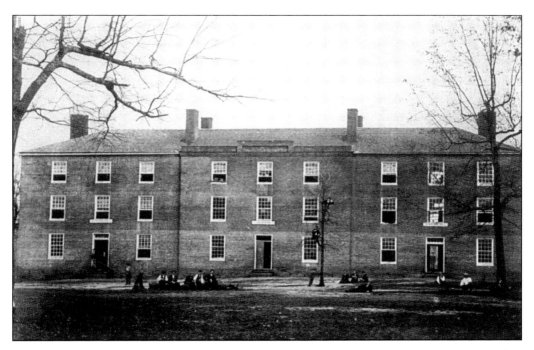

The first two dormitories on campus were constructed at the same time as the Lyceum. They were occupied by the first class of students to enroll at the university in 1848. They flanked the Lyceum on either side, and in the late 1870s, verandas were added to the buildings, which gave them a Victorian-era look. A third dormitory was constructed in 1857 because of the increase in student enrollment.

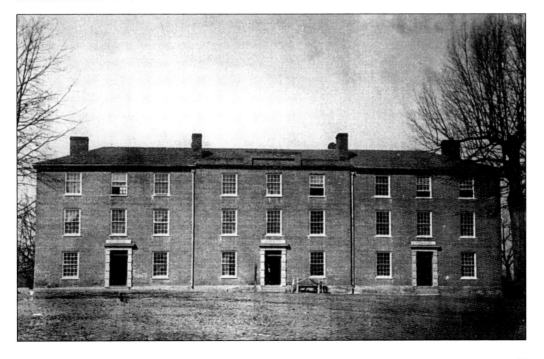

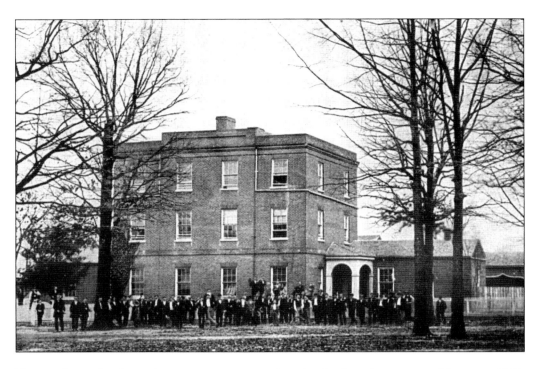

Two residences for the professors were constructed on the Circle and were opened for use in 1848. As part of the compensation to the professors, a residence on campus was provided. Each building flanked the student dormitories.

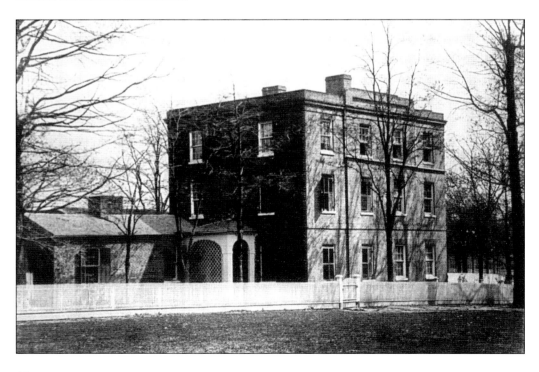

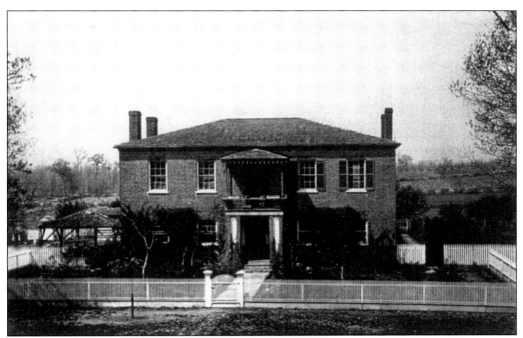

The original Steward's Hall was constructed at the same time as the Lyceum, the student dormitories, and the professors' residences in the first group of buildings constructed on campus. This building was directly behind the Lyceum in the area of the present-day J. D. Williams Library.

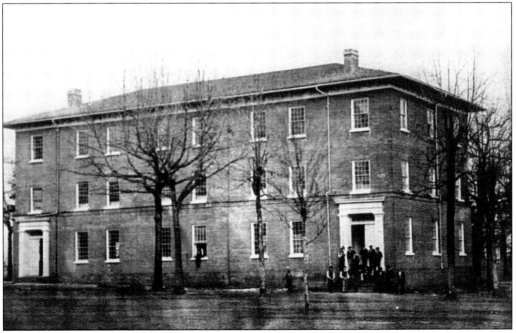

The chapel is the second oldest building to survive to the present day. The building was constructed in 1853 and was used, at various times, as a chapel, classrooms, the offices of the YMCA, and today the Croft Institute of International Studies.

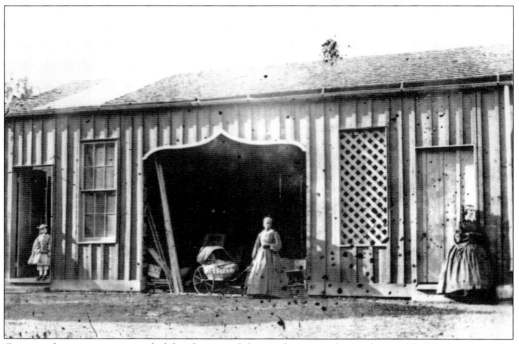

Carriage houses were provided for the use of the professors and were located behind each of the professors' residences. They were constructed in 1857.

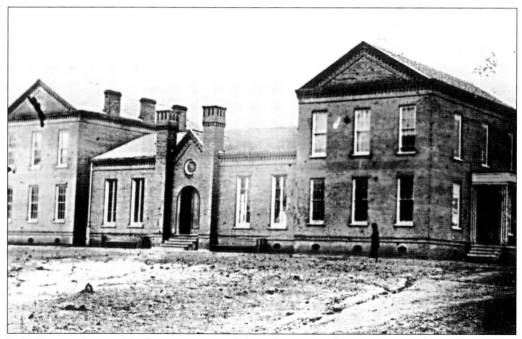

In 1857, a new Stewart's Hall was constructed when the current dormitories proved to be inadequate. The students paid between $10 and $12 per month for housing in this building.

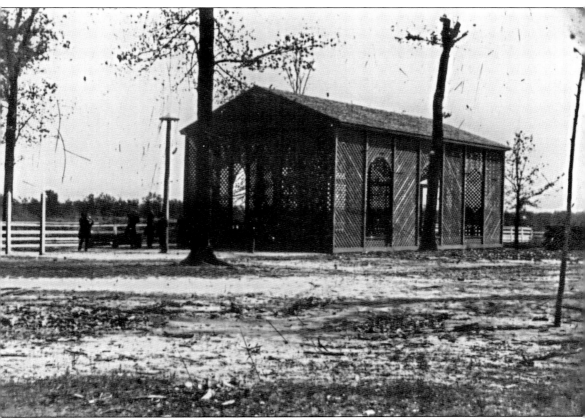

In 1859, chancellor F. A. P. Barnard felt the students needed a gymnasium to house the physical education equipment of the university. The building was a roofed lattice-work structure 60 feet long and 36 feet wide.

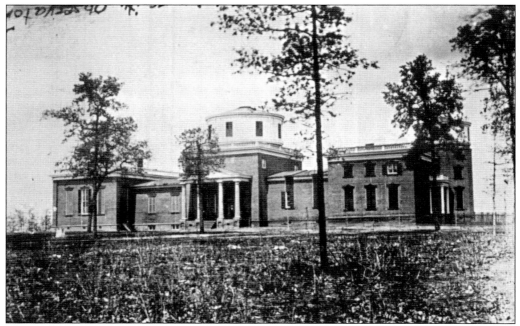

Chancellor F. A. P. Barnard had a plan to make the University of Mississippi one of, if not the best of, America's scientific universities. To this end, in 1859, he designed and had constructed an observatory to house the largest telescope in the United States. The building is the third oldest building on campus and was designed in the shape of an H, with the building facing true south. The central dome was intended for the large telescope. The smaller domes on both wings were intended for a comet seeker and a smaller telescope. Because of the beginning of the Civil War, the company that constructed the lens would not deliver the telescope to the university. It is now housed at Dearborn Observatory at Northwestern University.

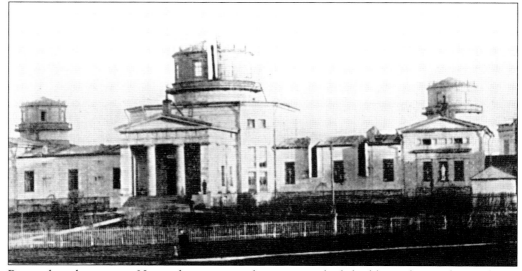

Barnard made a trip to Harvard to view its observatory, which had been designed to replicate the Poulkovo Observatory in St. Petersburg. The Russian observatory had been constructed in 1839, and this building was destroyed by Nazi bombs in 1941.

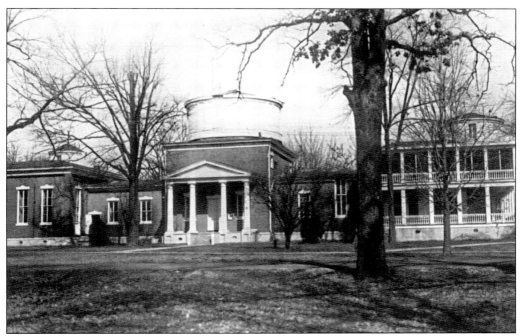

In later years, a sleeping porch was added to the observatory building when the residence of the chancellor was housed in the east end of the building. This sleeping porch has been removed.

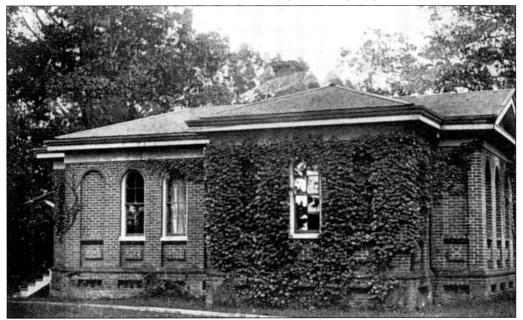

Chancellor Barnard also had a magnetic observatory constructed near the main observatory building in 1859. The building was for the study of terrestrial magnetism and meteorology in cooperation with the American Coast Survey. The building was used as a morgue during the Civil War when the campus was used as a hospital by both Union and Confederate forces. It later became known as the Dead House.

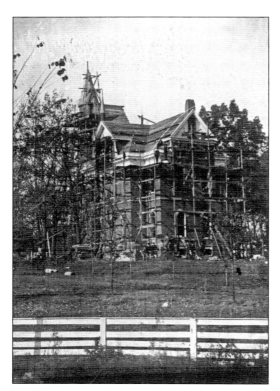

In 1889, chancellor Edward Mayes had a new library constructed on campus at a cost of $12,000. Prior to 1889, a portion the Lyceum served as a library. This building, now known as Ventress Hall, has at various times served as the law school, the geology building, and classrooms, and now houses administrative offices. It is the fourth oldest building on campus.

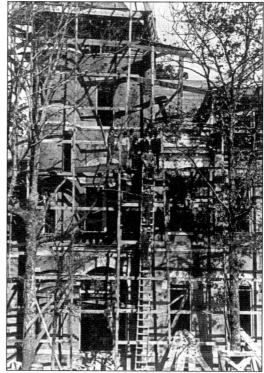

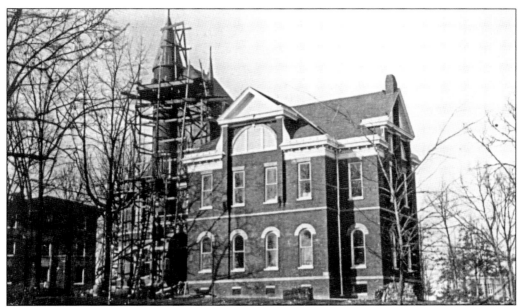

The Delta Gamma Sorority and the Alumni Association had Tiffany and Company of New York design and construct a stained-glass window in memory of the University Greys and other units that had members from the university. The University Greys were a unit of the Confederate Army composed of former students of the university that lost most of its members at the Battle of Gettysburg. The window is on the back of the building on the staircase leading to the upper floor. The dedication on the window reads, "Cum pietate alumnorum: In honor of those who, with ardent valor and patriotic devotion in the Civil War, sacrificed their lives in defense of principles inherited from their fathers and strengthened by the teachings of their Alma Mater, this memorial is lovingly dedicated." It should also be noted that soon after the building was constructed, students and returning students of the university started writing their names on the staircase wall leading up the turret of the building. These signatures remain there today.

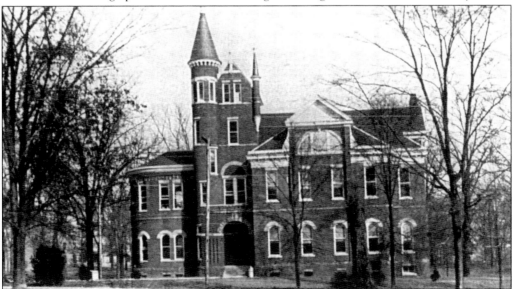

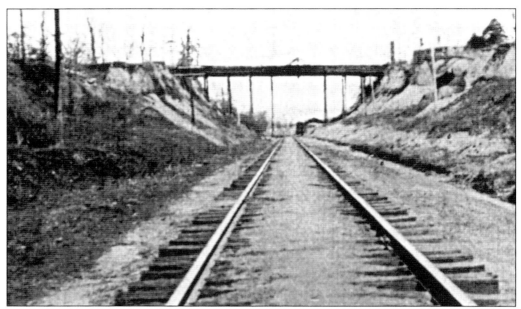

In 1857, the Mississippi Central Railroad was brought through Oxford from Grand Junction, Tennessee, to Canton, Mississippi. The railroad bed was constructed between the university and the town. There was a hill south of the depot, and a cut was dug through so that the train would be able to move out from the station. The cut became known as the Hilgard Cut, named for Prof. Eugene Hilgard, who later became the father of soil science.

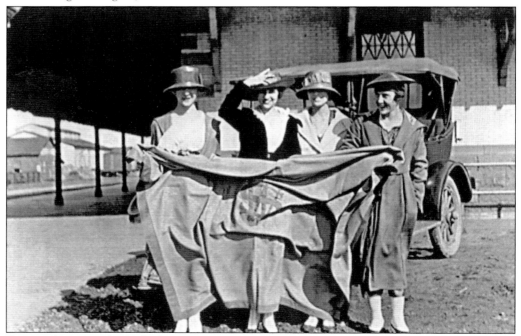

Four coeds wait at the Oxford University Depot for an arriving train. The students used the trains to come to Oxford for many years because of the poor highway system in Mississippi. The train lines no longer come through Oxford.

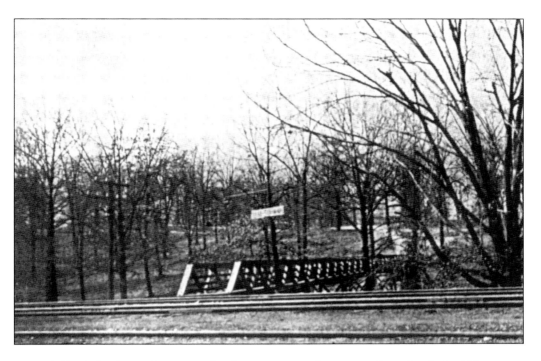

It was difficult for the students to make their way up to the campus from the Oxford University Depot. A bridge was constructed across a drainage ditch that led to a pathway up the hill to the campus. For the students' convenience, porters would meet each train, both in the morning and evening, to assist the students with their baggage.

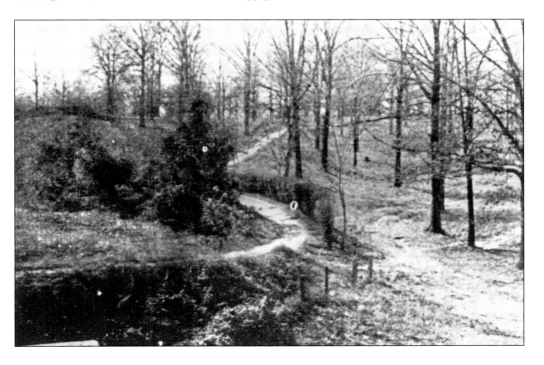

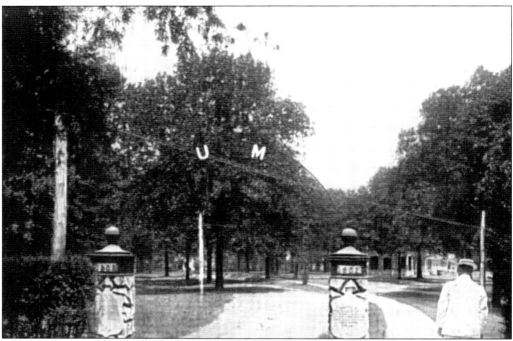

This is the entrance to the university on University Avenue. It was donated by the class of 1902. This entrance was just past the Hilgard Cut and is no longer in use.

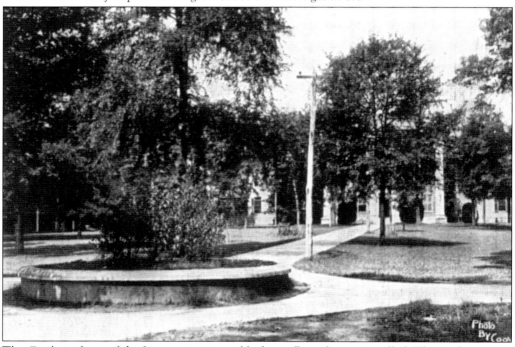

The Circle in front of the Lyceum is pictured before a flagpole was installed. This is the area in which the riots of 1962 occurred. On football game day, this area is also used by returning alumni and students for their tailgating.

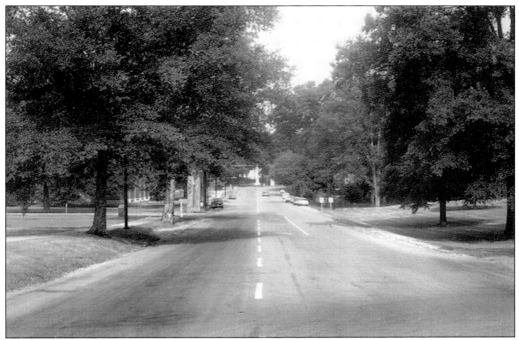

Present-day University Avenue leads to the Grove and the Circle on campus. The photograph was taken on the bridge that crosses the Hilgard Cut.

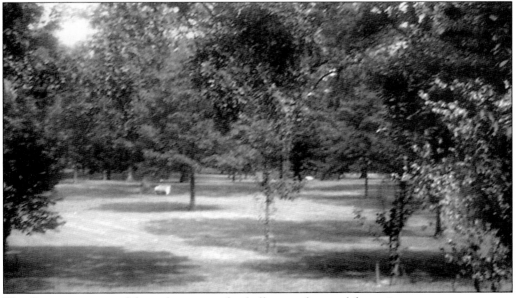

The Grove is now used for tailgating on football game days and for spring commencement on campus. The Grove has been used over the years for many campus events. During the Civil War, when the university was used for hospital purposes, tents were set up in the Grove to house injured Union and Confederate soldiers. In later years, movies were shown on a large screen erected in the Grove. Families would come to the free movies on campus and bring their lawn chairs or blankets to place on the ground.

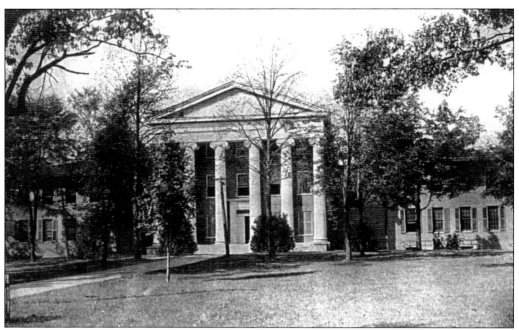

Wings were added to both sides of the Lyceum around the dawn of the 20th century. This photograph depicts the look of the Lyceum as it appears today.

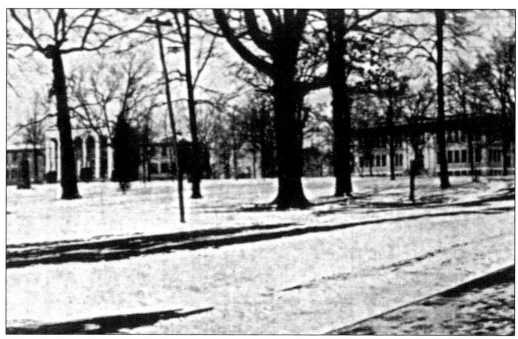

Ricks Hall, the first women's dormitory, was constructed in 1903. It was named in honor of Fanny Ricks, who contributed the funds for the construction. The dormitory was nicknamed "the Coop" and was located on the present-day site of the Student Union Building. The approximately 40 coeds who occupied the building in 1904 paid $9.50 a month for room and board.

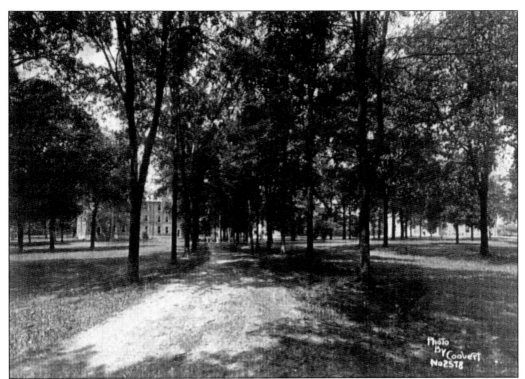

The Circle, which the Lyceum and other buildings face, is on campus near the world-famous Grove. Note that there was a dirt road leading to the Lyceum.

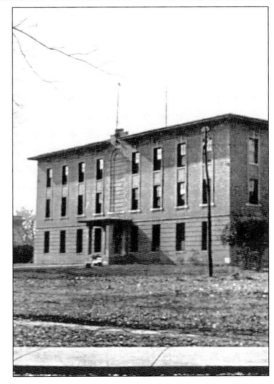

The first women's dormitory at the university was named for Fanny Ricks, whose philanthropic donation of $1,500 per year helped support summer terms at the university from 1900 to 1903.

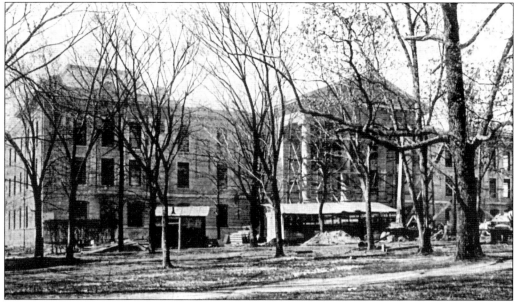

The men's dormitories that were built in 1848 began to be replaced in 1909 with the construction of Gordon Hall. The building was named in honor of Col. James Gordon, a veteran of the Civil War and a graduate of the university. He also served as the president of the alumni association. This building burned in 1934, and in the mid-1950s, the site was used for the construction of Carrier Hall, the School of Engineering building.

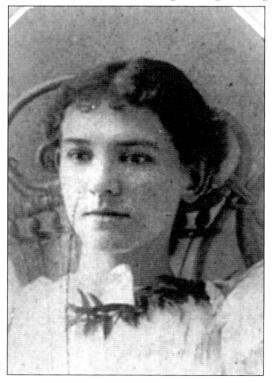

In the late 1890s, the students decided the university needed a yearbook. The first book was printed in 1897, and the yearbook staff needed a name. Students were asked to submit their ideas to the staff, and Elma Meek came up with the name Ole Miss. In the antebellum days, the master of the plantation's wife was nicknamed "Ole Miss" and any female children were called "young miss." Meek submitted the name, and it became the title of first yearbook. The name was later applied to the University of Mississippi.

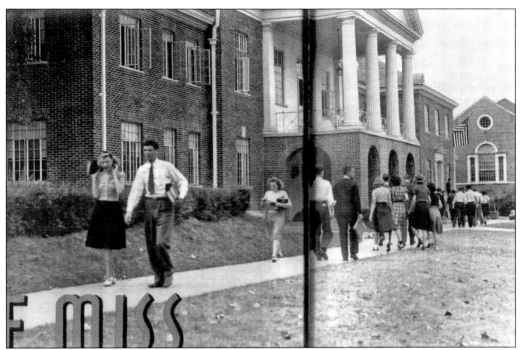

Prior to the building of the new Student Union Building, the campus post office, bookstore, and on-campus restaurant facilities were housed in Weir Hall. The on-campus restaurant was fondly called "the Grill." The building also housed an on-campus men's clothing store owned by Carl Coers.

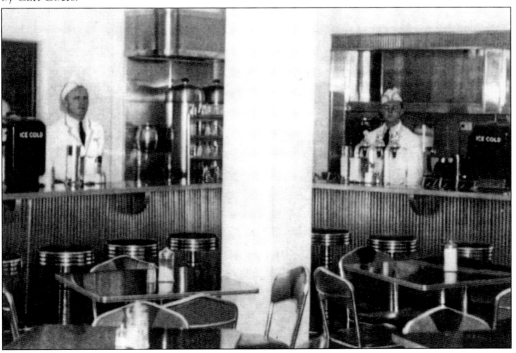

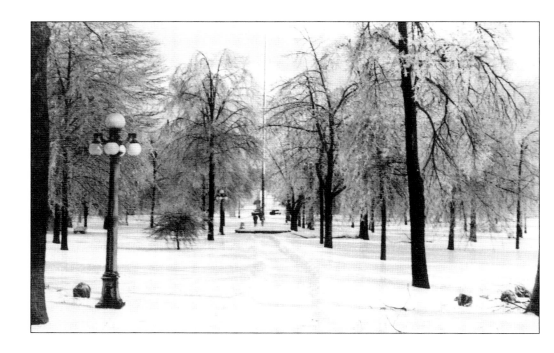

In the early 1950s, Ole Miss and Oxford experienced a rare heavy snowfall. The Circle leading from the Lyceum to University Avenue became very hard to navigate by the students coming to and from the campus. (Courtesy of Lauren Childress.)

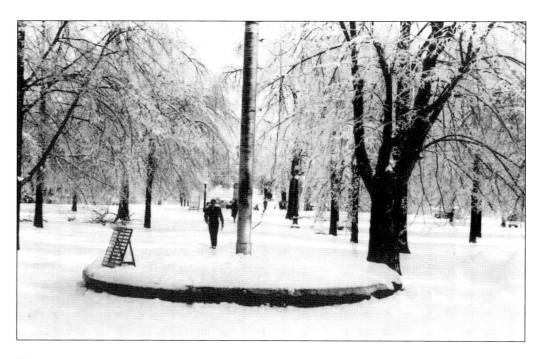

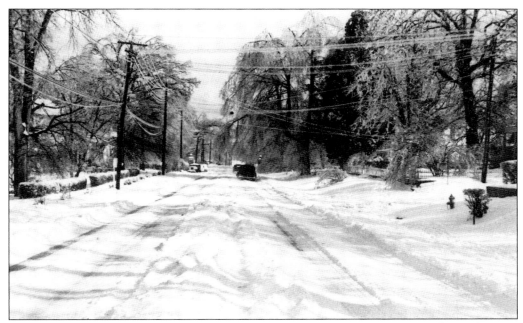

The early-1950s snowstorm blocked University Avenue and made it difficult for students to make their way to the campus. As with most small Southern towns, a heavy snowfall can bring movement to a halt. (Courtesy of Lauren Childress.)

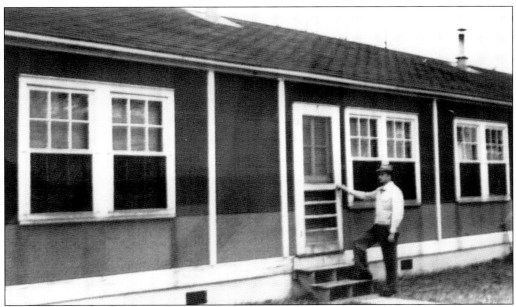

After World War II, returning married GIs who took advantage of the GI Bill had to have living facilities. The university recycled old army buildings for use as veterans housing. The area of the Tad Smith Coliseum near the nine-hole golf course became known as Vets Village. The buildings were also used for housing for campus employees as part of their salary from the university. (Courtesy of Lauren Childress.)

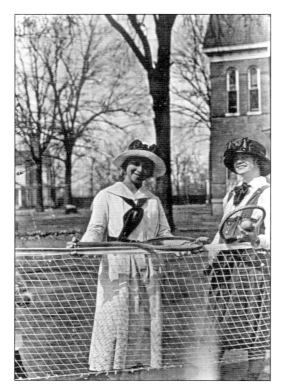

Before concrete tennis courts were constructed on campus, the Grove and its level grassy areas were used by the students to play tennis. Ventress Hall is in the background behind the coeds, who are preparing to play a match.

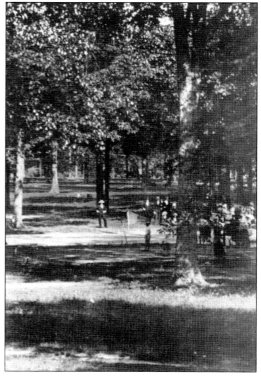

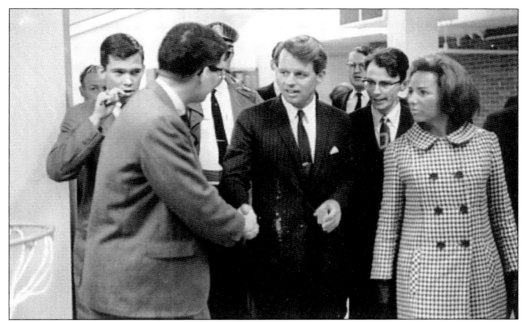

On March 18, 1966, Sen. Robert F. Kennedy and his wife, Ethel, came to the University of Mississippi. The senator was invited by the law school to come to the campus for a speech in Fulton Chapel. Due to the large number of people, more than 5,000, who wanted to hear RFK speak, the venue was changed to the Tad Smith Coliseum.

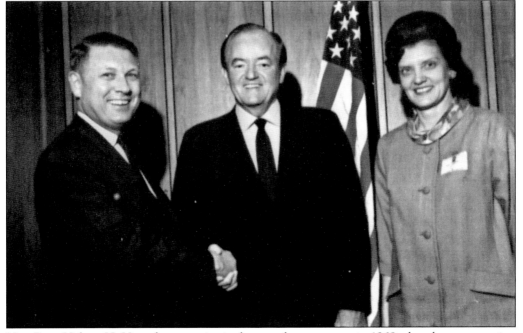

Vice Pres. Hubert H. Humphrey was invited to speak on campus in 1968 when he was running for president of the United States. He is shown with chancellor Porter L. Fortune and his wife, Elizabeth.

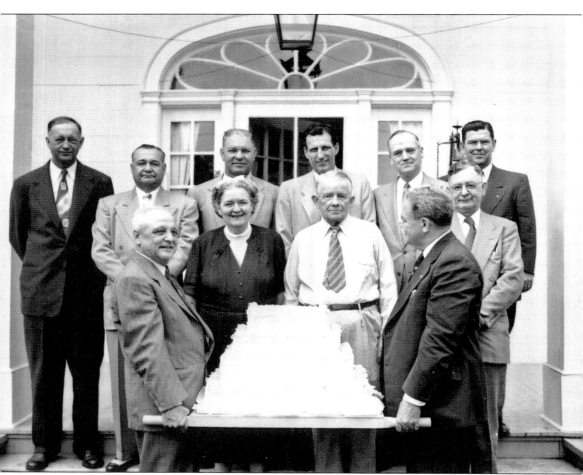

In 1955, lumberman Robert Carrier and his wife, Lenore, made two donations to the University of Mississippi. One was for the construction of the School of Engineering building that bears his name. The other was for the endowment of the Carrier Scholarships. Carrier, who was a major contributor to the university's athletic program, gave $500,000 for the establishment of the scholarship program. The first Carrier Scholar was Mary Ann Mobley, the first of three Ole Miss coeds to become Miss America. The Carrier home, located on campus, was willed to the university for use as the chancellor's home. Pictured from left to right are (first row, holding the cake) Chuck Trotter and Mayor R. X. Williams; (second row) Lenore Carrier, Robert Carrier, and T. E. Avent; (third row) A. H. Avent, Shine Morgan, coach Johnny Vaught, Dean Kellogg of the School of Engineering, Jeff Ham, and vice chancellor ? Haygood.

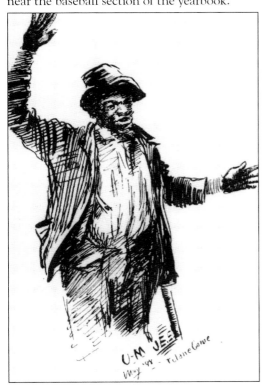

In the spring of 1896, "Blind" Jim Ivy wandered into the Ole Miss baseball park during a game with the Texas Longhorns. He asked if the Ole Miss team was winning and was told they were not. He began to cheer, in his loud booming voice, for the team. The baseball players rallied and came from behind to beat the Longhorns. With this event, he became a mainstay on the Ole Miss campus. In the 1898 Ole Miss yearbook, Blind Jim is shown in a photograph and a drawing near the baseball section of the yearbook.

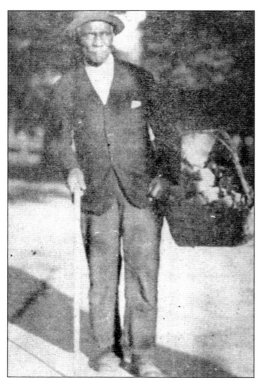

Blind Jim Ivy became known as the unofficial "Dean of Freshmen" for the university. Each fall, he would stand on the steps of the Lyceum and greet the new students on campus. He would remind them what was expected of them on campus. He was the only vendor allowed to sell peanuts and pencils in the lobby of the Lyceum. Students would take up contributions to buy Ivy a new suit each year. Some students would even take him to football games, where he would lead cheers for the Rebels. He was quoted as saying that he "never saw Ole Miss lose a game." It has been said that he was the model for Colonel Rebel, the unofficial Ole Miss mascot. Ivy died in 1955, and many students attended his funeral.

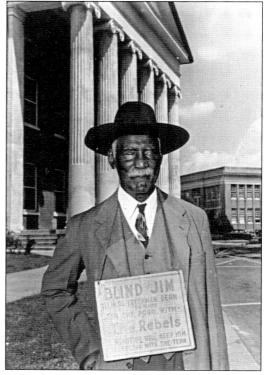

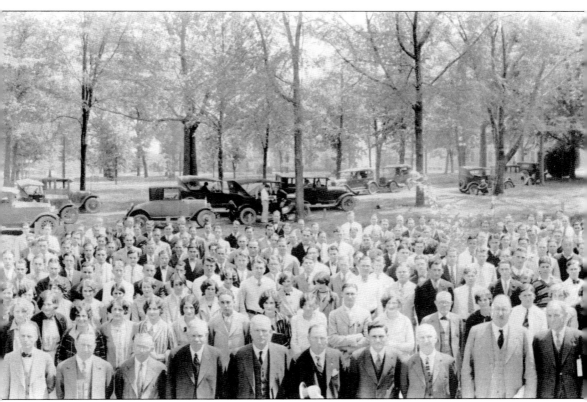

In 1927, a photographer came to Oxford and the university to make panoramic pictures of the town and campus. This photograph is the entire student body and faculty of the University of Mississippi. The photograph was taken in front of Peabody Hall on campus just to the right side of the Lyceum.

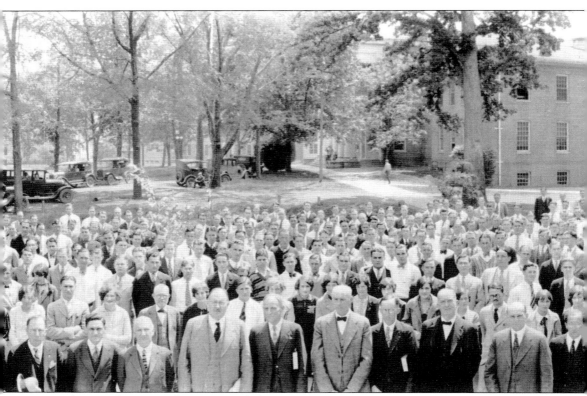

This is the second section of the panoramic photograph taken on the Ole Miss Campus in 1927.

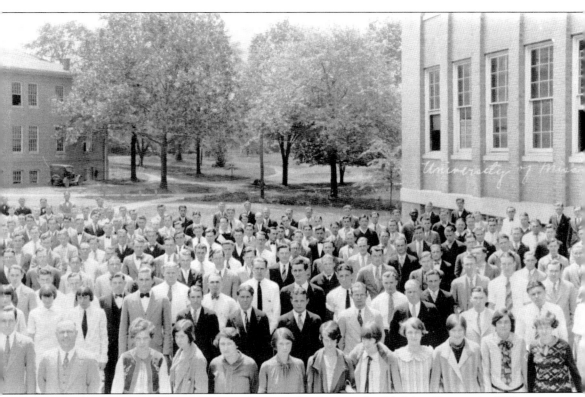

This is the third section of the panoramic photograph taken on the Ole Miss Campus in 1927.

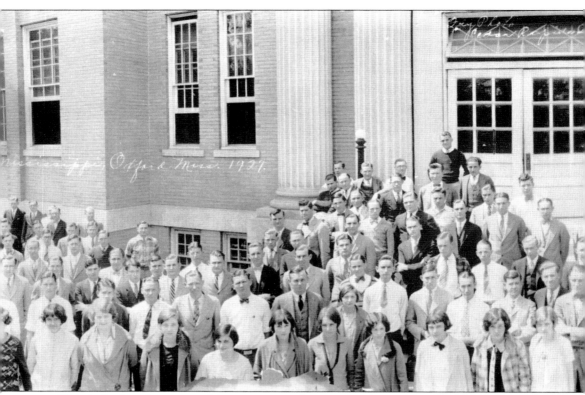

This is the fourth section of the panoramic photograph taken on the Ole Miss campus in 1927.

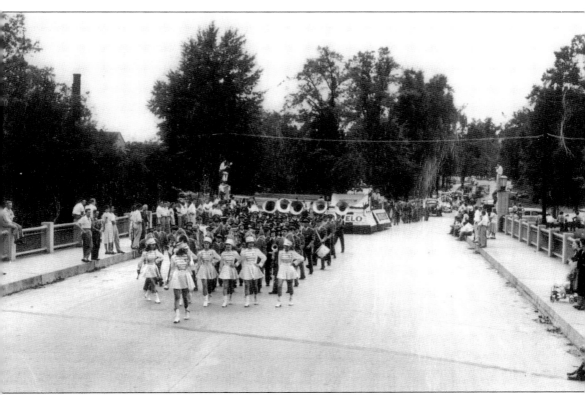

On the centennial of the University of Mississippi in 1948, Oxford and the university community had a parade from the campus to the Square. The parade made its way down University Avenue, crossing the Hilgard Cut to the Square. This is the Tupelo High School band along with a float from their hometown. (Courtesy of Will Lewis.)

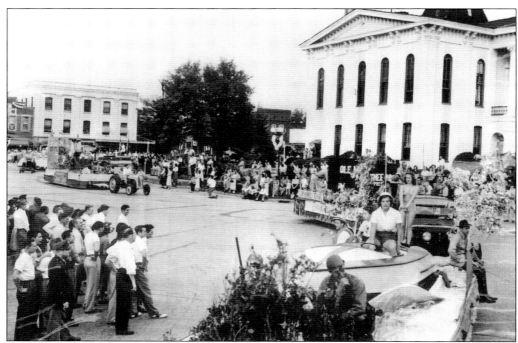

The 1948 Ole Miss Centiennial Parade makes its way around the Square. Ann Kay Burrow is in the boat, and Amy Jo Cole is waterskiing.

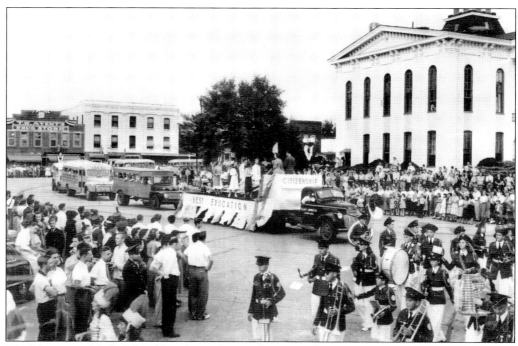

The University High School band marches in the 1948 Ole Miss Centennial Parade.

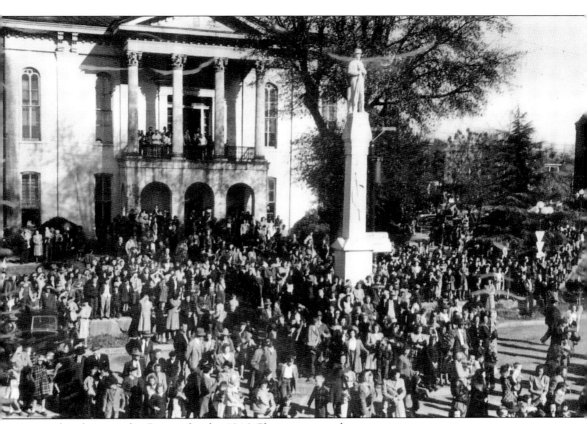

A crowd gathers on the Square for the 1946 Christmas parade.

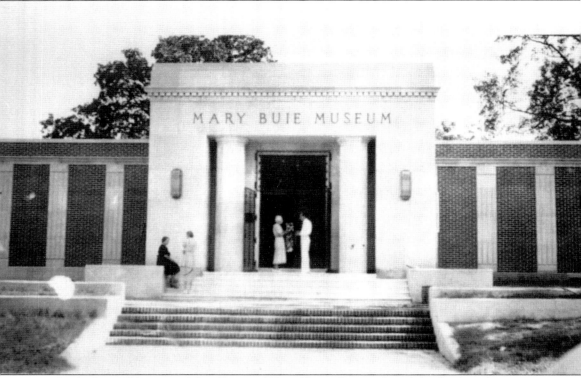

In the late 1930s, sisters Mary Buie and Kate Skipwith contributed the funds to form a museum for the city of Oxford. The sisters were world travelers and wanted a place to house the many artifacts they had collected from their tours and other sources. Kate Skipwith is shown with Will Lewis Sr. in the doorway at the 1939 dedication of the building. In later years, the City of Oxford gave the museum to the university, and it formed the anchor for the Porter Lee Fortune Cultural Center. The cultural center is composed of the museum; William Faulkner's home, Rowan Oak; the Walton-Young Home; the Kate Skipwith Teaching Museum; the Ford Center; and Barnard Observatory.

Four

CITY OF OXFORD HISTORICAL SCENES

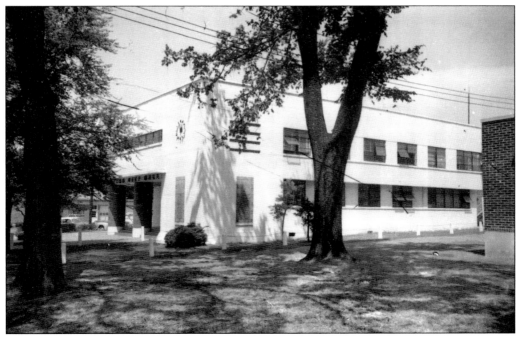

In the 1930s, Oxford constructed a new city hall and fire station on Jackson Avenue at the corner of North Ninth Street. This property was later traded to the federal government for the Federal Building on the Square, built in 1885, which became the new city hall. This site is now the new Federal Building and Federal Courthouse.

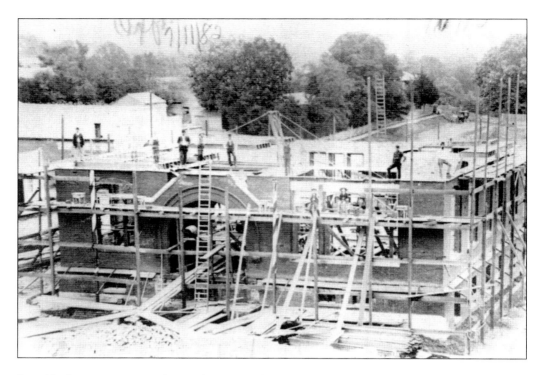

In 1883, the construction of a new $50,000 Federal Courthouse and post office was begun on the Square in Oxford. The site was where the University Hotel had stood, which was destroyed by the Union Army when the town was burned on August 22, 1864. Behind the building, a cotton gin stood for a number of years.

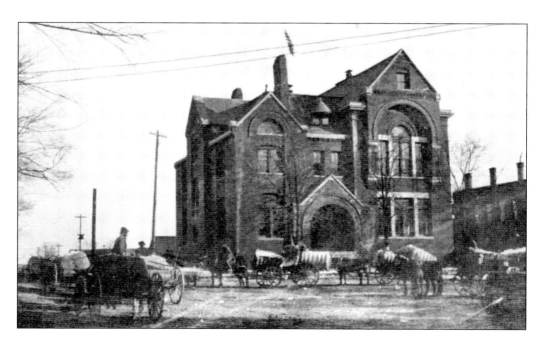

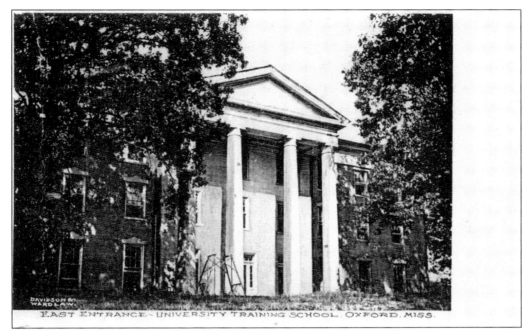

EAST ENTRANCE~UNIVERSITY TRAINING SCHOOL, OXFORD, MISS.

Oxford has always been the seat of learning for this part of Mississippi. One of the first schools was the Union Female College, which would later be sold and converted to the Oxford Female Academy. The property on South Eighth Street and Fillmore Avenue was purchased by the University Training School in 1904 and became a male academy. This school would remain in existence until 1911, when the building burned.

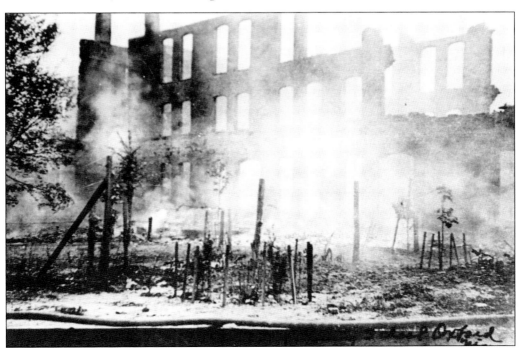

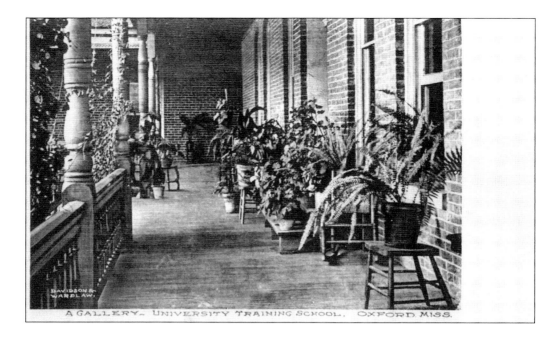

A GALLERY - UNIVERSITY TRAINING SCHOOL, OXFORD MISS.

The University Training School, which had operated since the 1840s as either a female or male academy, had a large building just off University Avenue on South Eighth Street. These two postcards from the stationery shop of Davidson and Wardlaw depict the beauty of the school and its verandas. It must have been a pleasant place to study for the students who would board at one of the schools over the years.

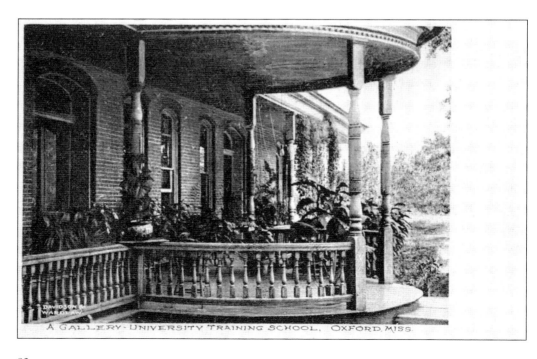

A GALLERY - UNIVERSITY TRAINING SCHOOL, OXFORD, MISS.

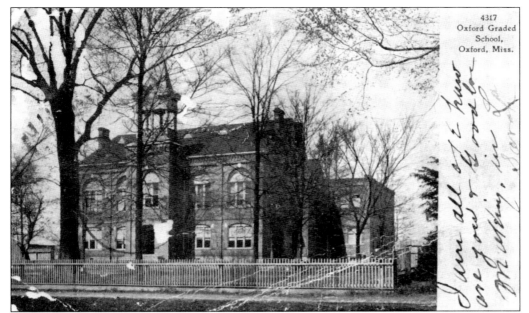

4317
Oxford Graded
School,
Oxford, Miss.

Oxford has provided for public education since the late 1800s. The Oxford Graded School was located on Jackson Avenue on the property now housing the Federal Building. Several additions were made to the school property over the years, and the school housed grades one through seven until the early 1970s, when several new schools to house facilities for elementary education were constructed. The playground was located behind the school building, which was torn down in 1946 and replaced with a building that was used until the 1970s.

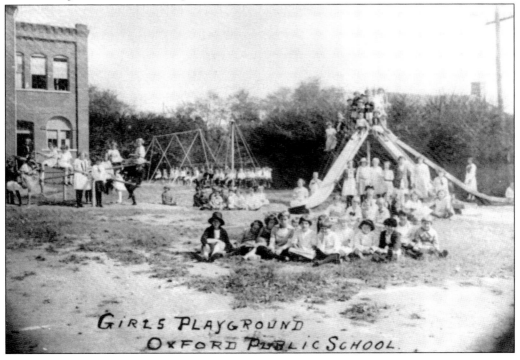

GIRLS PLAYGROUND
OXFORD PUBLIC SCHOOL.

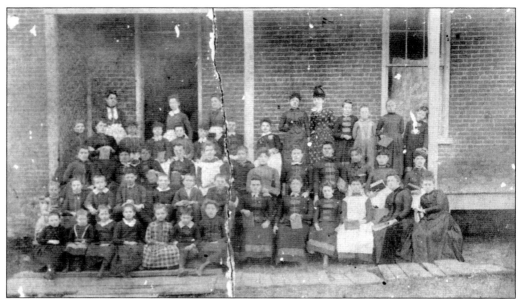

Students of the Union Female Academy pose for this photograph in the 1880s. The school was chartered in 1838 as the Oxford Female Academy, only one year after the founding of Oxford.

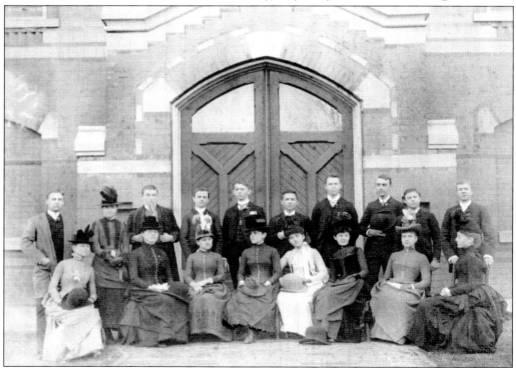

Young men and women members of the Cumberland Presbyterian Church pose for a photograph on the front steps of the church in the early 1880s. The church was located on South Lamar Boulevard between the present-day Harrison and Tyler Avenues on the west side of the street. The property is now occupied by several businesses, including Pearl Street Pasta.

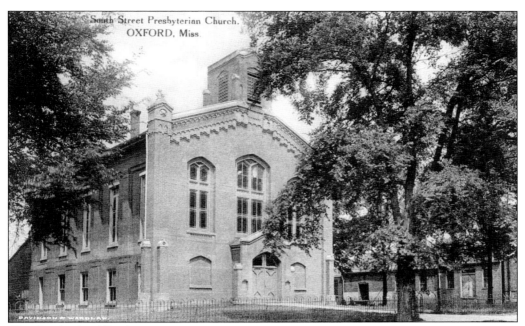

South Street Presbyterian Church.
OXFORD, Miss.

The Cumberland Presbyterian Church, also known as South Street Presbyterian Church, was considered by many the most beautiful church in Oxford. At the time of its use, it was the largest church building in Oxford and was used during the Civil War as a meeting place for the local citizenry. The building is also shown in the only photograph of the destroyed Oxford. It originally had columns on the front of the building that were removed, and the front facade was made to look more Victorian or Gothic.

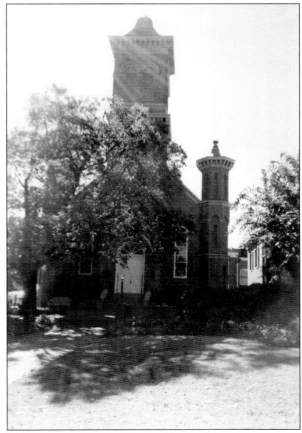

The First Presbyterian Church was incorporated in Oxford in 1837. The wood-frame church building was not burned in 1864 when Oxford was destroyed. The current church building was constructed after the war in 1881.

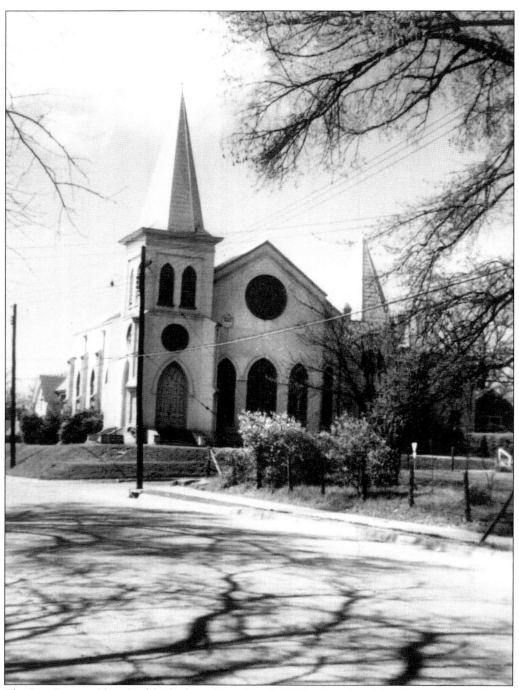

The First Baptist Church of Oxford was formed in 1842. The first church building was on Jefferson Avenue on the corner of North Thirteenth Street and was a log building. The building depicted here was constructed in 1882 and was located on the northwest corner of North Ninth Street and Van Buren Avenue. This building was torn down in 1952 when the new church building was constructed and occupied directly across the street.

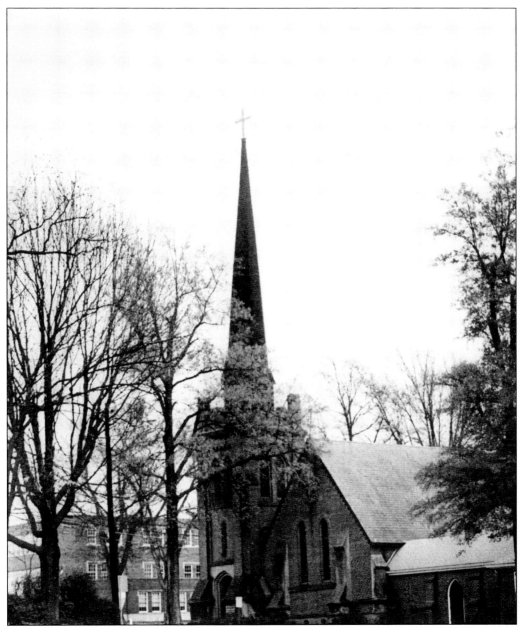

St. Peter's Episcopal Church was formed and the church building constructed in 1851 on its current site. This church building survived the burning of Oxford in 1864 and has been in use since its construction. Please note the old Oxford Elementary School on Jackson Avenue in the background.

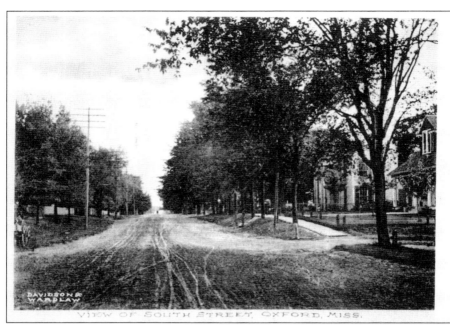

VIEW OF SOUTH STREET, OXFORD, MISS.

Two views of South Street before the street paving in Oxford in the early 1920s are pictured here. The Davidson and Wardlaw postcard above is looking south from the intersection with University Avenue, and the view below is looking north at the corner of Bucannan Avenue toward the Square. The name of South Street was changed to South Lamar Boulevard in honor of L. Q. C. Lamar. In the photograph above, a horse and rider are visible. Note the old streetlight hanging over the thoroughfare in the image below.

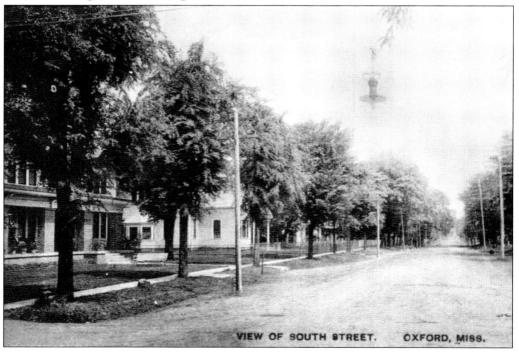

VIEW OF SOUTH STREET.   OXFORD, MISS.

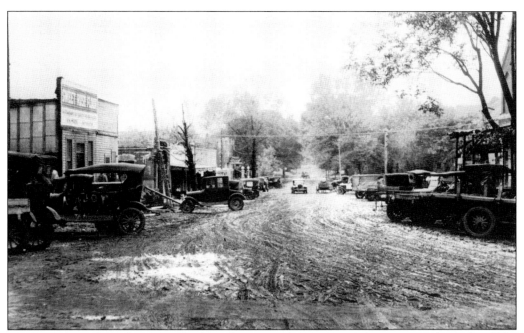

This is a view of South Lamar Boulevard prior to the paving of the street in the early 1920s. On the right-hand side of the photograph, one can barely see the corner of the Cumberland Presbyterian Church.

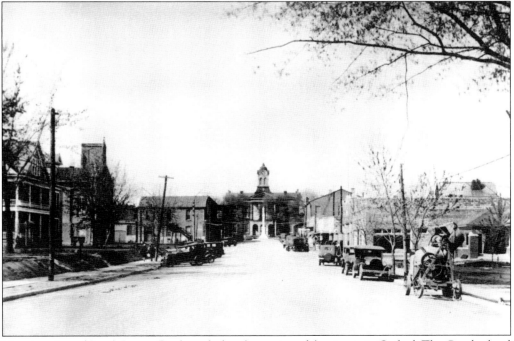

Here is a view of South Lamar Boulevard after the paving of the streets in Oxford. The Cumberland Presbyterian Church and the current 208 South Lamar restaurant can be seen on the left. The building on the far left of the photograph is where Holli's Sweet Tooth is now located.

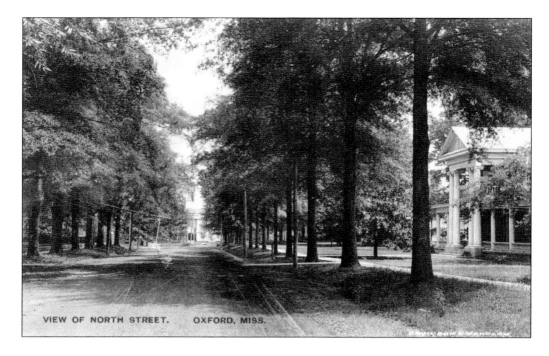

VIEW OF NORTH STREET. OXFORD, MISS.

Two views of North Street, later renamed North Lamar Boulevard, come from the Davidson and Wardlaw stationery shop. Both photographs are looking north toward the intersection with Price Street. Chancellor Augustus Baldwin Longstreet's home can be seen on the right in the above photograph. These postcards are dated before the paving of the streets in the early 1920s.

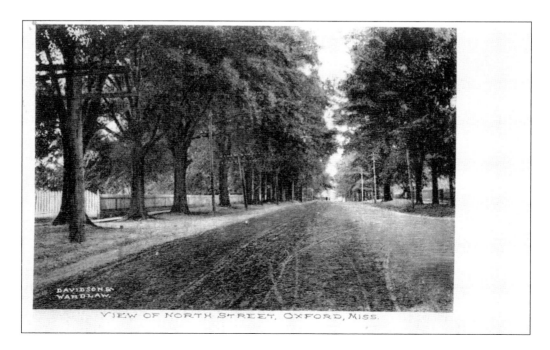

VIEW OF NORTH STREET, OXFORD, MISS.

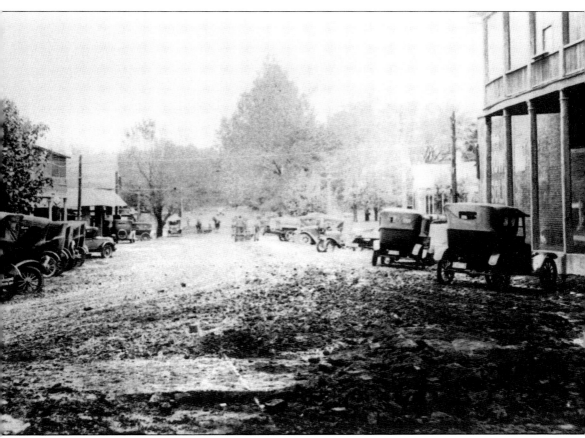

This photograph of North Street looking north from the Square dates prior to the paving of the streets. The building with the veranda is the current location of the First National Bank.

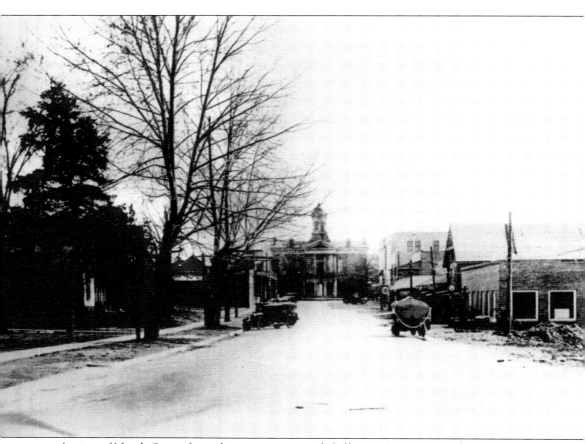

A view of North Street from the intersection with Jefferson Avenue was taken after the paving of the street in the early 1920s. Note the building on the right-hand side of the photograph is the current location of the Boure Restaurant.

Five

AROUND THE TOWN AND COUNTY

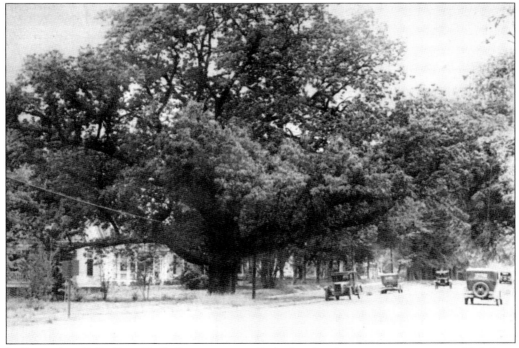

In December 1862, Gen. U. S. Grant came to Oxford on his first attempt to capture Vicksburg by following the Mississippi Central Railroad from Grand Junction, Tennessee. While in Oxford, he used Cedar Oaks as his headquarters on North Street. At that time, Cedar Oaks was on the northeast corner of the intersection of North Street and Jefferson Avenue. This tree was located across the street, and Grant would meet his commanders under the tree. It was given the name the "Grant Oak."

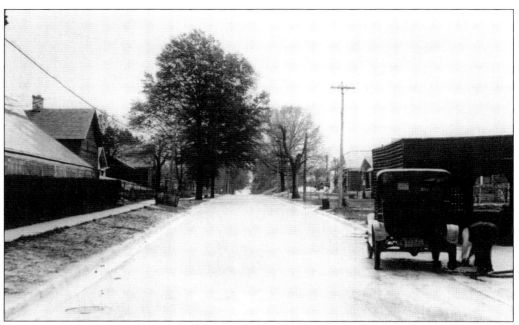

At one time, the owner of the antebellum mansion Cedar Oaks owned the Oxford Floral Company. His greenhouse was adjacent to his home on North Lamar Boulevard at the corner of Jefferson Avenue. This photograph shows the greenhouse on the left looking toward St. Peter's Cemetery. It looks as though the man on the right is fixing a flat on his automobile.

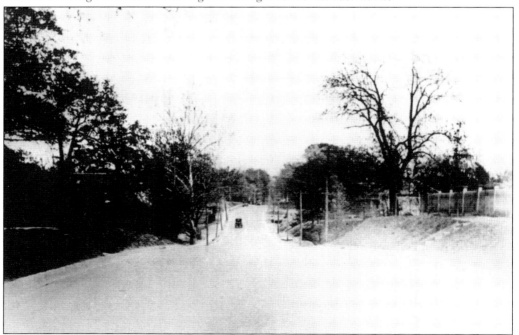

This is University Avenue at its intersection with South Fifth Street looking east. The fence on the right-hand side of the photograph was once around the home of Kate Skipwith, which is now the Kate Skipwith Teaching Museum.

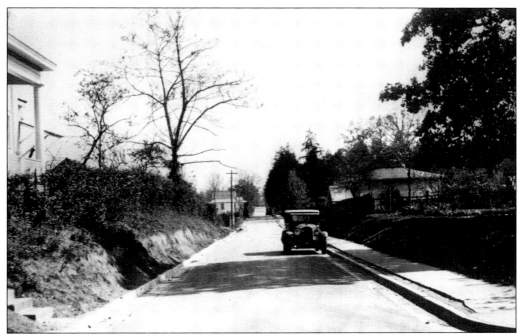

In this photograph of the corner of South Eleventh Street and University Avenue, William Faulkner's paternal grandfather's home can be seen on the left. Faulkner would walk this street from Rowan Oak to the Square to visit his mother, who lived around the corner.

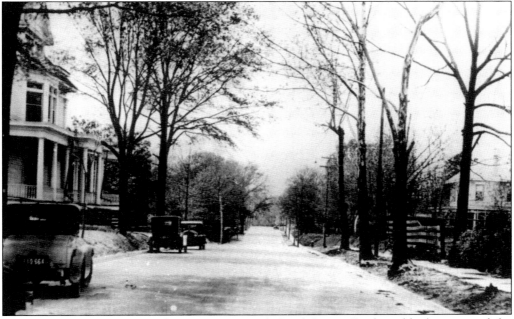

This is University Avenue at the intersection with South Lamar Boulevard looking toward the University of Mississippi campus. The home visible on the left-hand side of the photograph belonged to William Faulkner's grandfather Col. J. W. T. Falkner. The home was moved in 1930 to face University Avenue in lieu of facing South Lamar Boulevard.

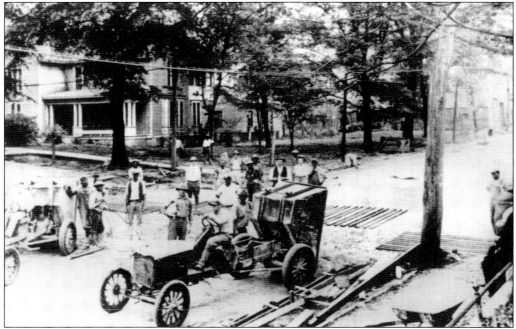

A paving crew works to pave Van Buren Avenue at the corner of North Ninth Street in the early 1920s. The home on the left side of the photograph was demolished to make way for the annex to St. Peter's Episcopal Church.

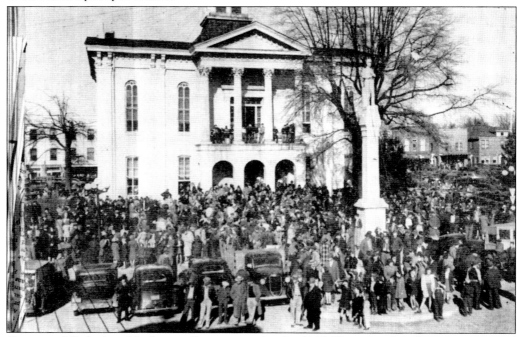

Citizens of Oxford and Lafayette County wait for the 1946 Christmas Parade to come around the south side of the Square. In the upper left, one can see the Christmas lights that used to be strung from the courthouse clock to the buildings around the Square.

The Brown and Goodwin Commissary was located on the southeast side of the Square. The photograph dates from about 1927. This building and its interior was used in scenes from the movie of William Faulkner's book *Intruder in the Dust*, filmed in Oxford in 1949. The building now houses Off-Square Books and is used for the *Thacker Mountain* radio program and for readings by authors who come to Oxford to sell their books.

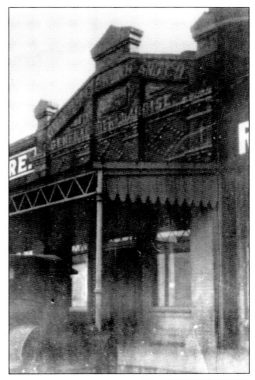

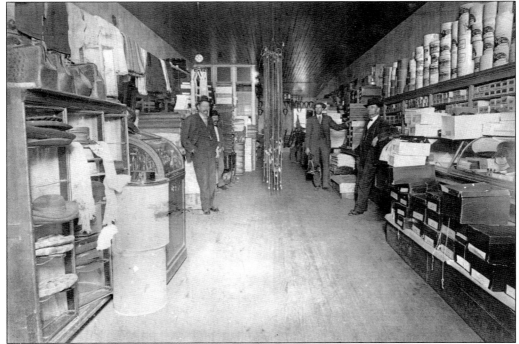

The interior of the Brown and Goodwin Commissary is pictured here. The men in the photograph are, from left to right, Billy Goodwin, J. B. Brown, Frank Heard, and Pete Ramey.

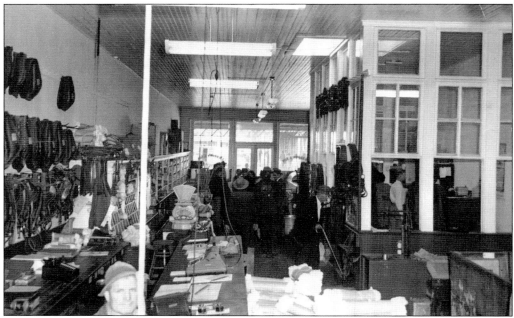

A later photograph shows the interior of the Brown and Goodwin Commissary after the name was changed to J. B. Brown and Son. This business's name was changed when J. B. Brown purchased his partner's interest in the 1920s. His son, W. Ross Brown, came into the family business in 1926. The original business was formed in 1898.

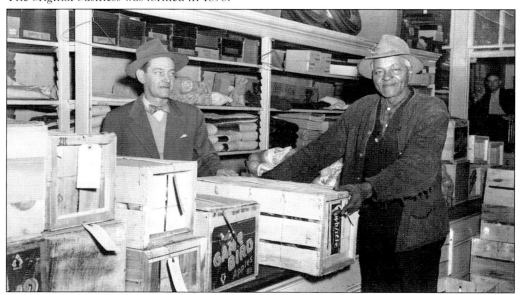

W. Ross Brown, the father of Patricia Brown Young, continued a tradition in the late 1940s that his father had started many years before for the farmhands who worked on his considerable land holdings. Over 60 families would receive crates of fruit as a Christmas gift. Ira Ward, who had worked for Brown for more than 20 years, is shown picking up his crate of fruit. At the time, Brown did not remember when his father started the tradition, but it had become a part of his life as much as a Christmas tree.

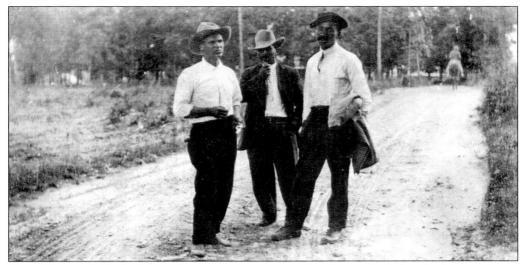

Sheriff Robert S. Black (left) is shown standing on a road leading to Oxford and talking with two local residents. Black was the Lafayette County sheriff in the late 1920s and early 1930s. The grip of his pistol can bee seen hanging out of his pocket.

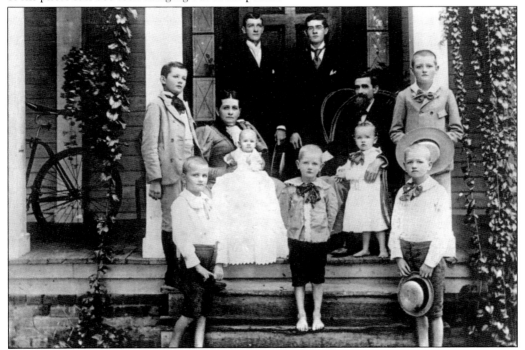

The George Washington Leavell family is shown on the front porch of their home on North Sixteenth Street. Corra Berry Leavell gave birth to nine boys, who all attended Ole Miss from the 1890s until the first part of the 20th century. The Leavell boys were Landrum Pinson (1874–1929), Arnaud Bruce (1876–1949), James Berry (1880–1957), George Wayne (1882–1957), Frank Hartwell (1884–1949), Leonard O. (1886–1963), Clarence Stanley (1886–1968), Roland Quinche (1891–1963), and Ullin Whitney (1894–1963). All nine sons and their wives, along with their father and mother, have markers at or are buried in St. Peter's Cemetery.

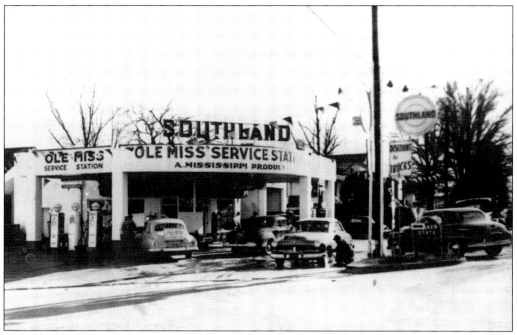

The Ole Miss Service Station was located on the southeast corner of South Lamar Boulevard and University Avenue. The photograph is from the early 1950s. BanCorpSouth is now located on the site.

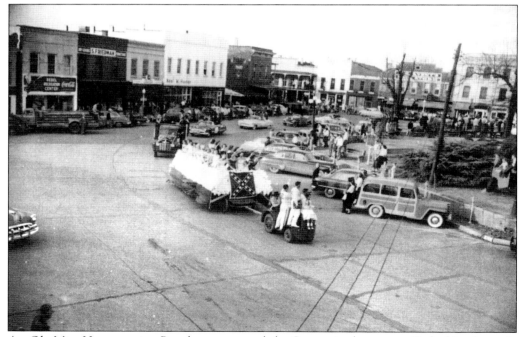

An Ole Miss Homecoming Parade goes around the Square in downtown Oxford in the early 1950s. This is the west side of the Square looking toward the Downtown Grill. The photograph was taken from the veranda of what is now Square Books.

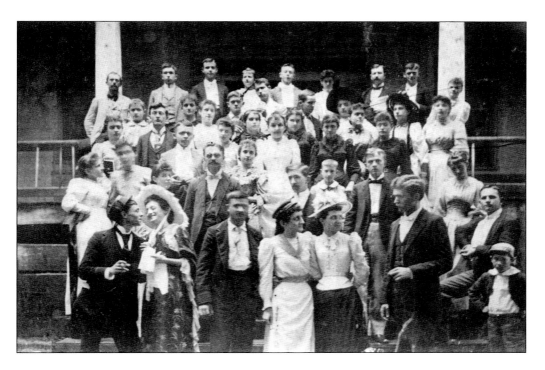

The Lafayette Springs Hotel was a favorite gathering place during the last part of the 19th century and the beginning of the 20th century. The hotel was popular for its mineral baths on the property. Note the "jug band" in the photograph below.

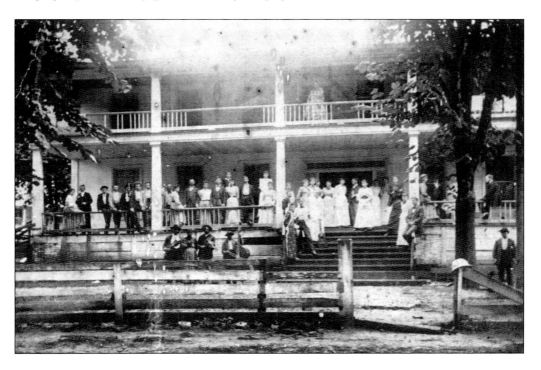

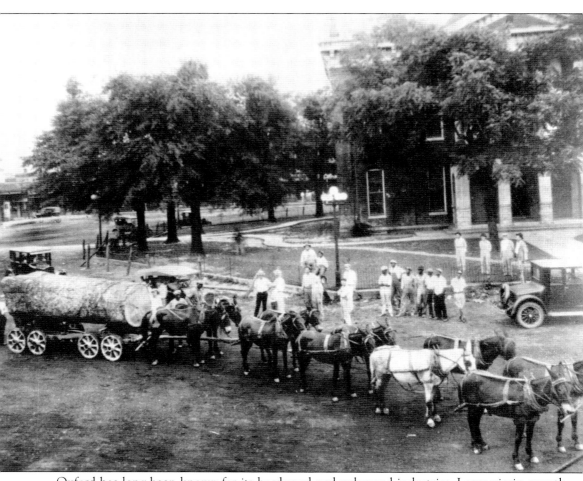

Oxford has long been known for its hardwood and pulpwood industries. Large virgin-growth hardwoods have been cut for many years in the river bottoms, such as the Yocona or Yellow Leaf bottoms, and other areas of the county.

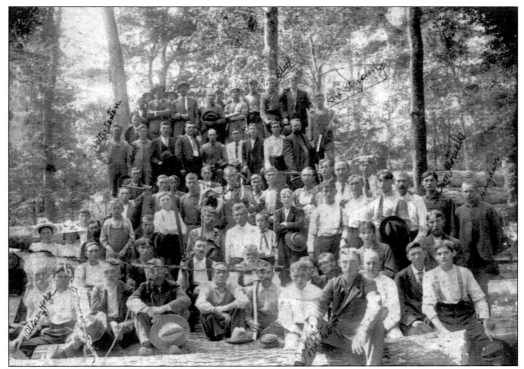

The local woodcutters were known as "peckerwoods." They would move their sawmill on skids from place to place to cut wood into usable boards. The sawmill was powered by steam.

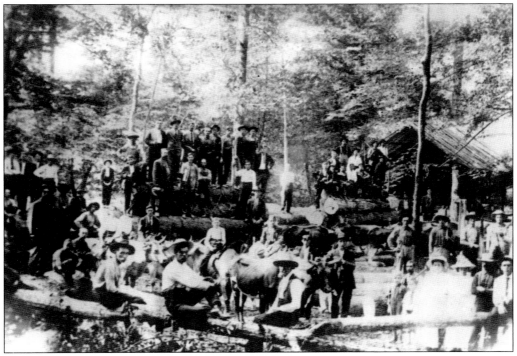

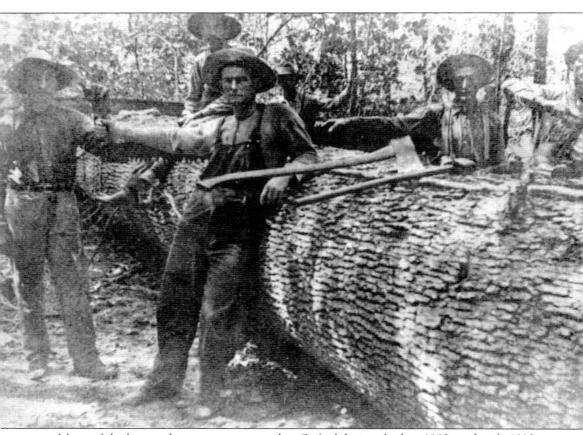

Many of the homes that were constructed in Oxford during the late 1880s and early 1890s were built from lumber that the "peckerwoods" cut in the river bottoms of Lafayette, such as Yellow Leaf Creek bottom. The lumber would be cut by their portable sawmill and delivered to Oxford by wagon.

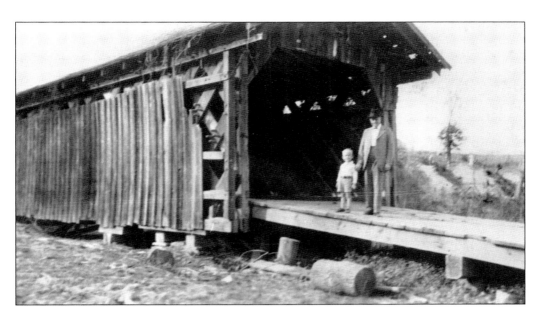

Covered bridges are not normally seen in the South, but these bridges are an exception. Both of the bridges were over the Yocona River that is in the southern part of Lafayette County.

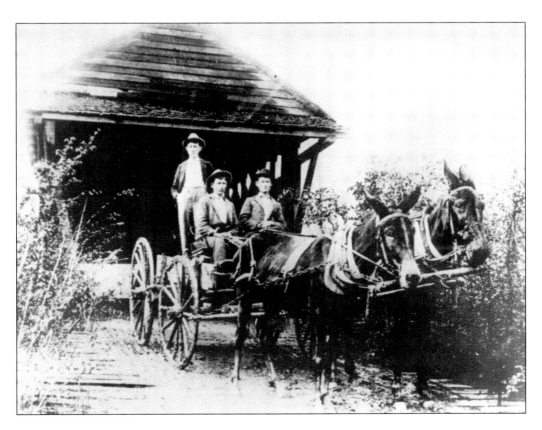

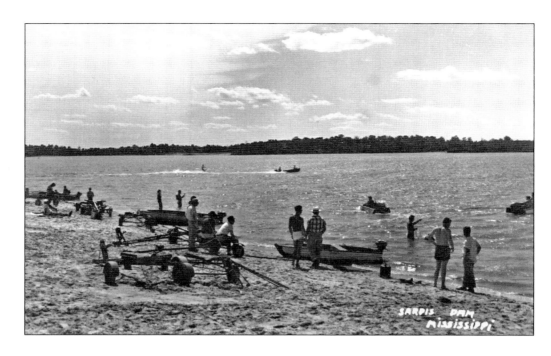

The Sardis Reservoir was constructed as relief for flooding in the Mississippi Delta by a WPA project in the 1930s. This was one of four reservoir projects constructed around the same time. The Enid, Arkabutla, and Grenada Reservoirs were the other three. This part of the lower lake was known as Rebel Beach.

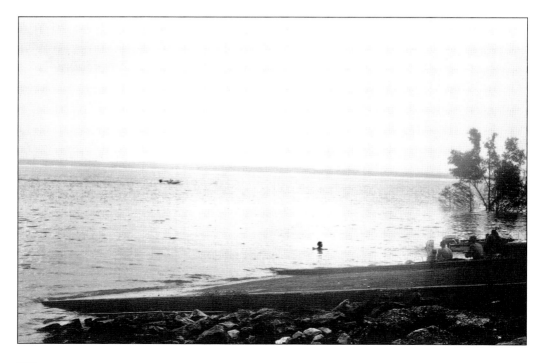

Six

Oxford's Most Famous Resident, William C. Faulkner

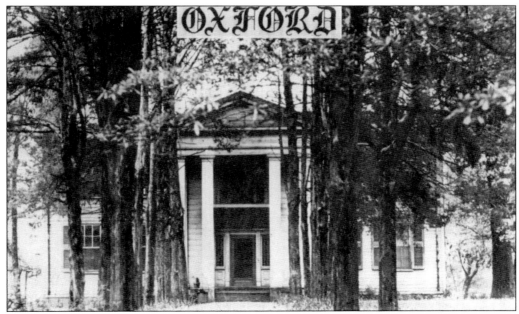

Oxford became the home of William Faulkner's grandfather J. W. T. Falkner's family a number of years before 1900. J. W. T. was the first to come to Oxford, and his son Murry would move his family to Oxford in 1903 when young William was only five years old. Faulkner would purchase his antebellum mansion in the early 1930s. He would give the name Rowan Oak to the old Sheegog mansion. He would remain in this home, except for a short stay in Virginia to be near his daughter Jill, until his death in 1962.

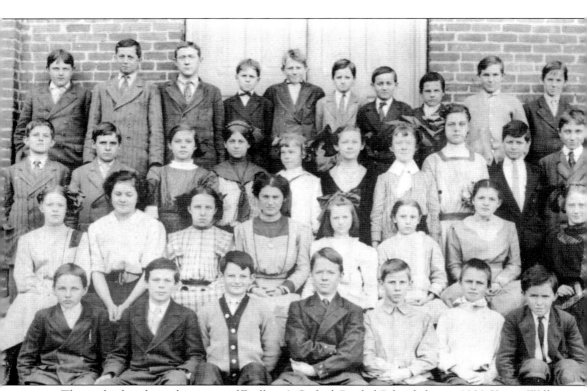

This is the fourth-grade picture of Faulkner's Oxford Graded School class in 1909. Young William is the fifth boy from the right in the fourth row.

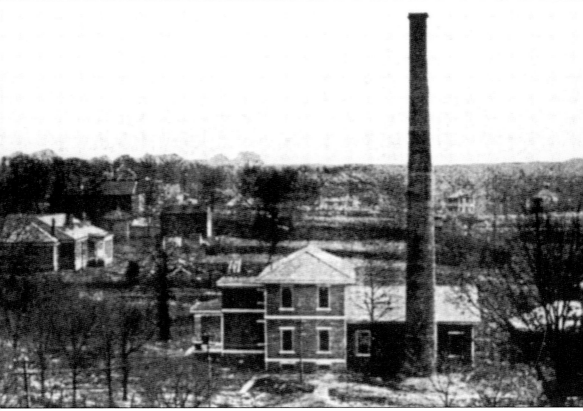

After his marriage to Estelle Oldham in 1929, William and his bride would rent an apartment in the home of Elma Meek on University Avenue. Meek was a student at the university when she proposed the name Ole Miss for the yearbook. While living there, William had a night job at the Ole Miss power plant. It was said he would use the time at work to write *As I Lay Dying*. This photograph looks north from Vaught-Hemingway Stadium toward the Grove.

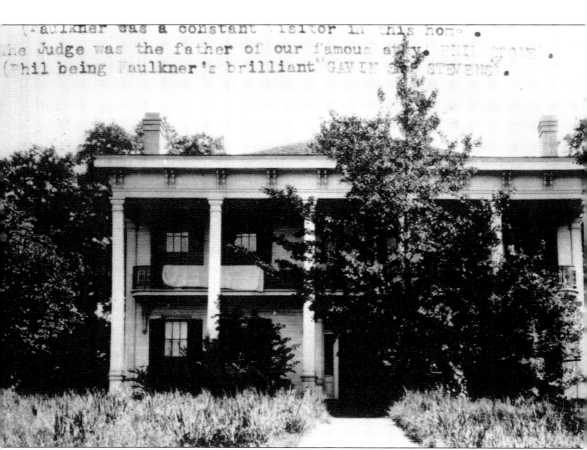

Faulkner's closest friend in Oxford was attorney Phil Stone. Faulkner was a frequent visitor to the Stone home on Washington Avenue. Stone's father, who was also an attorney, had an extensive library that Faulkner would use constantly. The Stone home burned in the 1940s, and a city recreation center is now on the site across from the local park commission swimming pool. It is said that Faulkner used his friend as the model for his fictional attorney, Gavin Stevens.

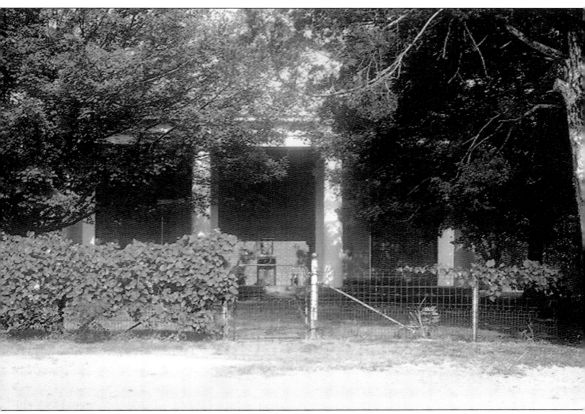

Because Faulkner's wife-to-be, Estelle Oldham, had been divorced, they could not be married in the local Episcopal church they attended. He then asked Dr. W. D. Hedleston, who was a University of Mississippi professor and pastor of the College Hill Presbyterian Church, to marry them. Some Faulkner scholars report they did not marry in the church but were married on the front porch of the church. Other accounts are that they married in the church, and still others say that they were married at Hedleston's home, Sunset Hill, just down the road from the church.

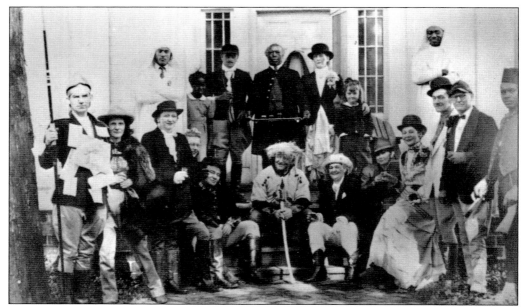

One of the more famous photographs of Faulkner, Estelle, and their Oxford friends is at a party they had at Rowan Oak. Faulkner was known to have a good sense of humor, and this is evident in these photographs. It was a costume party, and the above photograph has been seen in many books on Faulkner. Patricia Brown Young's mother and father were lifelong friends of the Faulkners and were at this party. Note the man on the left-hand side of both photographs. He has mail attached to his clothes to denote that he is a knight wearing a suit of mail, which was flexible body armor.

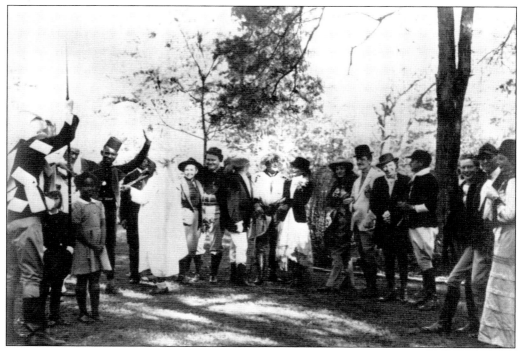

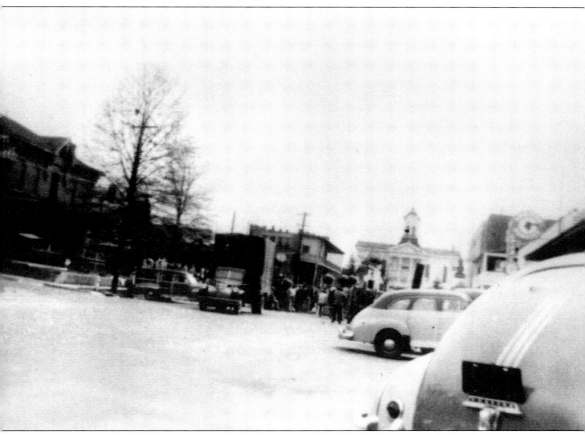

Oxford was the site of the filming of a movie based on Faulkner's novel *Intruder in the Dust* in 1949. The Lafayette County Jail was the scene of many shots during the film and is on the left-hand side of this photograph.

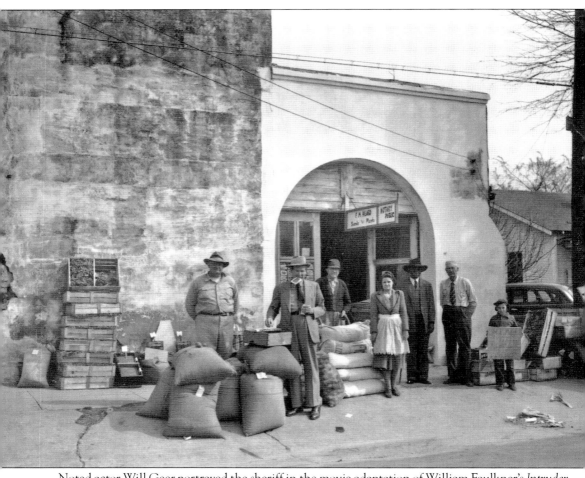

Noted actor Will Geer portrayed the sheriff in the movie adaptation of William Faulkner's *Intruder in the Dust*. He is shown (second from left) at Heard's Feed Store just off the Square behind city hall on East Jackson Avenue. F. M. Heard is standing second from right next to "Blind" Jim Ivy. The area is now a city-owned parking lot.

Noted black actor Juano Hernandez played Lucius Beauchamp, who is accused of murder in *Intruder in the Dust*. He is shown above with local Oxford residents near the staircase going up to the veranda over what is now Rooster's on the Square. The office of Gavin Stevens, who saves his life, was located at the top of the stairs overlooking the Square. Hernandez is shown below during the filming walking by Claude Jarman Jr., who played the young Jefferson baseball player in the movie. The University High School baseball team players were used as extras in the movie. Many other Oxford residents were also used as extras in the movie.

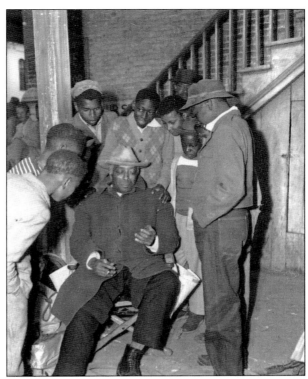

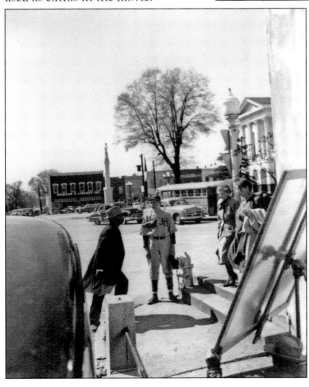

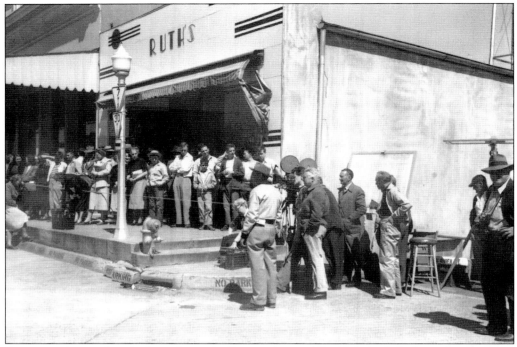

Scenes are being shot for *Intruder in the Dust* in front of Ruth's ladies' clothing shop, next to Neilson's on the Square. Note the local residents of Oxford standing around to watch the filming of the movie.

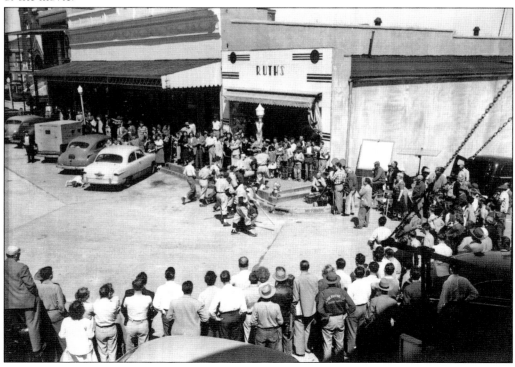

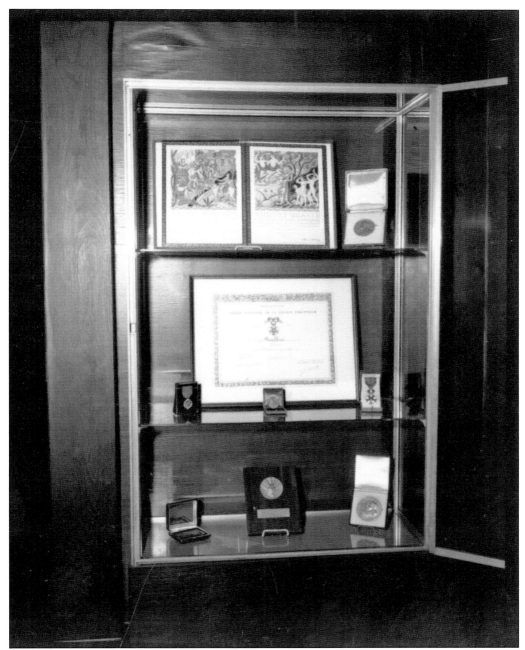

This is the showcase holding Faulkner's Nobel Prize for Literature and other awards he received during his lifetime. These awards can be viewed in the Special Collections at the University of Mississippi's J. D. Williams Library. Also in the viewing area are movie posters for the movies that have been made from Faulkner's works and volumes of his books, which have been printed in many languages.

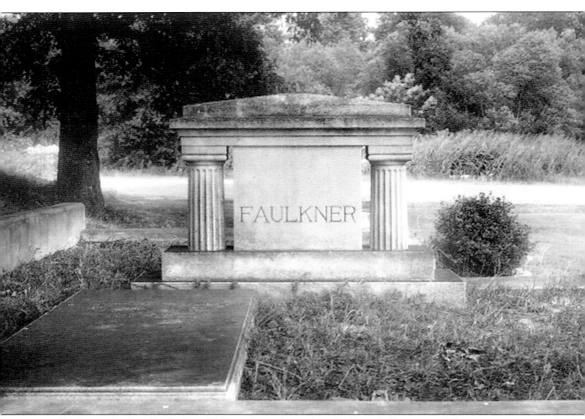

Faulkner died in Oxford in 1962 and was buried in St. Peter's Cemetery. There was no room for him in the Faulkner grave plot at the cemetery, so he was buried in a new area opened in the early 1960s. He was one of the first citizens of Oxford to be buried in this area, just off North Sixteenth Street. The land was formerly T. E. Avent's pea patch. Many visitors to Oxford go by his burial plot, and in honor of Faulkner, they leave a bottle of whiskey for him.

Seven

PRESERVING OUR
HERITAGE

Lucius Quintus Cincinnatus Lamar was born at the old Lamar homestead in Putnam County, Georgia, on September 17, 1825. He moved to Oxford with his wife, Jenny Longstreet Lamar, in 1850 after his father-in-law, Judge Augustus Baldwin Longstreet, was made the second chancellor of the University of Mississippi. The renovation of his home in Oxford has been one of the projects of the Oxford–Lafayette County Heritage Foundation.

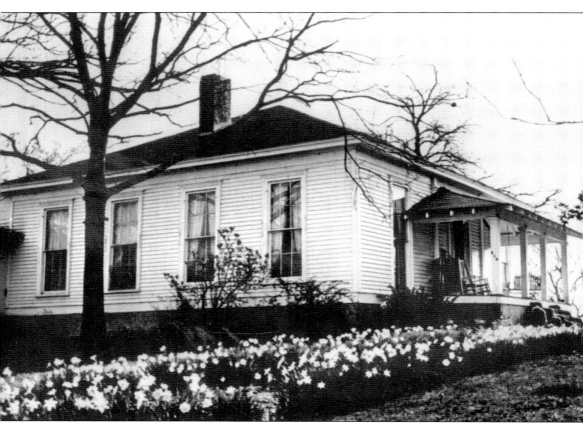

Lamar sold his home in Oxford after the death of his wife, Virginia Lafayette Longstreet Lamar, and moved to Washington, D.C., full-time when he was appointed associate justice of the Supreme Court by Pres. Grover Cleveland in 1888. Lamar is one of the few men in American history that has served in all three branches of the government of the United States. He was elected to Congress before and after the Civil War. He was later appointed a U.S. senator, and in 1885, he was appointed Secretary of the Interior in Cleveland's cabinet. This photograph was taken by noted Oxford photographer Col. J. R. Cofield in 1929.

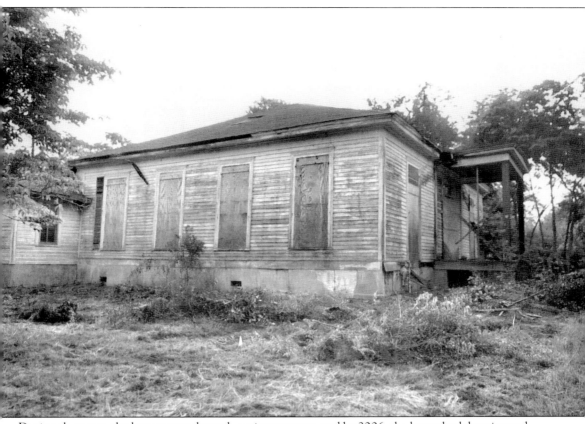

During the years, the home went through various owners, and by 2006, the home had deteriorated almost to the level of no return. The heritage foundation purchased the home with the help of Oxford's state representatives, Sen. Thad Cochren and Congressman Rodger Wicker, and the Mississippi Department of History and Archives.

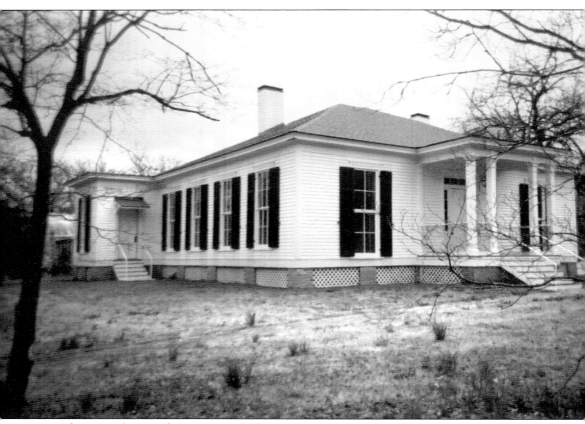

After several years of renovation, the home is now open to the public and is under the control of the City of Oxford. The home is used for traveling historical exhibits, and in the future, it will house exhibits of the life of Lamar.

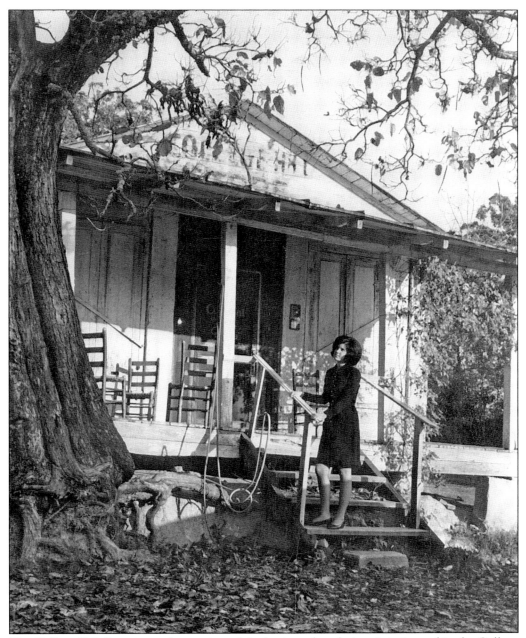

The College Hill Store is another project of the heritage foundation. It is situated in the College Hill community outside of Oxford. It is a prime example of the small Southern country store of the antebellum period. It houses a collection of antiques from Oxford and College Hill's early history and is open to the public for tours by appointment. The young lady in this photograph is Cynthia Vance, wife of Brooke Vance, who was the university's pilot. He was killed shortly after this picture was taken in a tragic crash of the university's airplane during a trip to Baton Rouge.

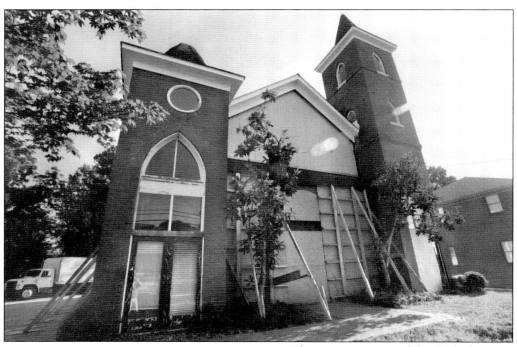

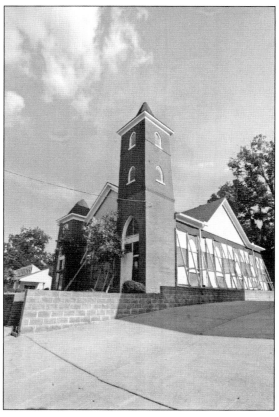

The current project of the Oxford–Lafayette County Heritage Foundation is the Burns Belfry, the first African American church built in Oxford after the Civil War. The original church building was constructed on West Jackson Avenue on the edge of Freedman's Town, which is where former slaves built their community after the war. It was replaced by the building under renovation in 1910. It was constructed by church members and served as the Burns United Methodist Church for many years. It was last used as the office of noted author John Grisham, and when he moved his home to Virginia, he donated the building to the heritage foundation for the use of the Oxford Development Association and the foundation as a multicultural museum and repository of the history of Oxford and Lafayette County. The author's proceeds from the sale of this publication will be used for the renovation efforts by the heritage foundation. Contributions can be made to the Heritage Foundation, P.O. Box 622, Oxford, MS 38655, a 501c nonprofit organization. The contributions are tax deductible.

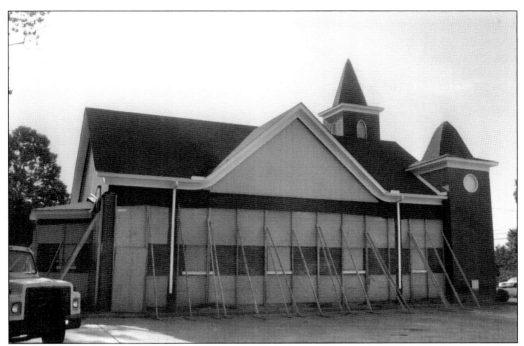

This is the east elevation of the Burns Belfry during phase one of the restoration. More than 1,200 metal anchors were used to attach the original brick veneer wall to the new wall structure inside the building.

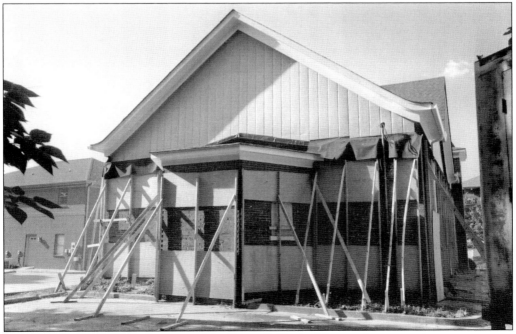

This is the rear, or south, elevation of the Burns Belfry building under restoration.

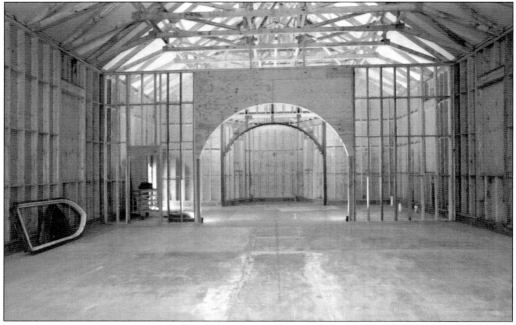

The phase one restoration of the Burns Belfry building included a new wall and roof structure. The interior wall will separate the auditorium from the back third, which will house a conference room, a catering kitchen, and two bathrooms.

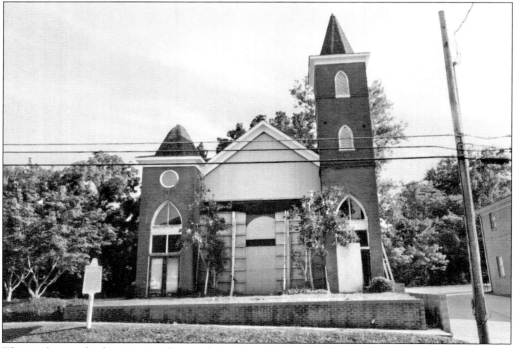

This is the north elevation, or front, of the Burns Belfry building under restoration.

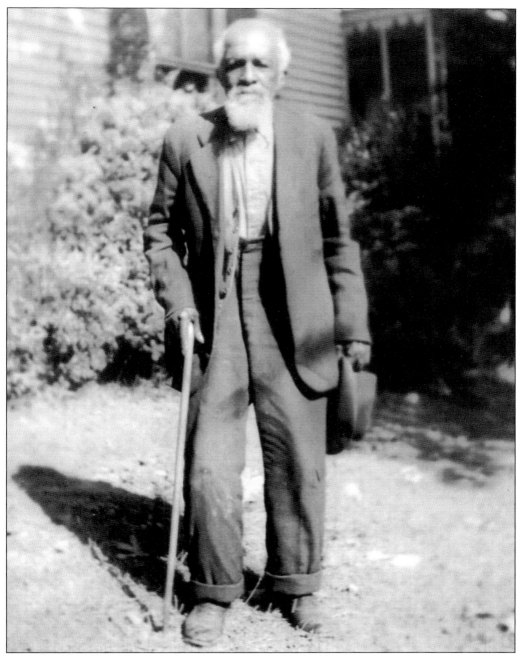

It is the intent of the heritage foundation and the Oxford Development Association to house any and all items relating to the history of Oxford and Lafayette County in the renovated Burns Belfry. This photograph and the story of the man depicted in the image are a prime example of the artifacts for the multicultural museum. Nick Tyson was the body servant for L. Q. C. Lamar, and as a young man, he followed Lamar into the Civil War. He is quoted as saying that he, at one time, held the reins of Gen. Robert E. Lee's horse, Traveler. At the time local Oxford resident Andrew Fox took this photograph in 1952, Tyson was 104 years old.

DISCOVER THOUSANDS OF LOCAL HISTORY BOOKS
FEATURING MILLIONS OF VINTAGE IMAGES

Arcadia Publishing, the leading local history publisher in the United States, is committed to making history accessible and meaningful through publishing books that celebrate and preserve the heritage of America's people and places.

Find more books like this at
www.arcadiapublishing.com

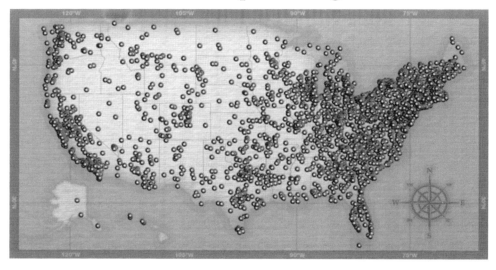

Search for your hometown history, your old stomping grounds, and even your favorite sports team.

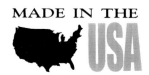